AUTHENTIC DIALOGUE
WITH PERSONS WHO ARE
DEVELOPMENTALLY DISABLED

of related interest

**Challenges to the Human Rights of People
with Intellectual Disabilities**
Edited by Frances Owen and Dorothy Griffiths
Foreword by Orville Endicott
ISBN 978 1 84310 590 9

**Guide to Mental Health for Families and Carers
of People with Intellectual Disabilities**
*Edited by Geraldine Holt, Anastasia Gratsa, Nick Bouras,
Theresa Joyce, Mary Jane Spiller and Steve Hardy*
ISBN 978 1 84310 277 9

**Working with People with Learning Disabilities
Theory and Practice**
David Thomas and Honor Woods
ISBN 978 1 85302 973 8

**Promoting Social Interaction for Individuals
with Communicative Impairments
Making Contact**
Edited by M. Suzanne Zeedyk
ISBN 978 1 84310 539 8

**Empowerment in Everyday Life
Learning Disability**
*Edited by Paul Ramcharan, Gwyneth Roberts,
Gordon Grant and John Borland*
ISBN 978 1 85302 382 8

AUTHENTIC DIALOGUE WITH PERSONS WHO ARE DEVELOPMENTALLY DISABLED

SAD WITHOUT TEARS

JENNIFER HILL

LEARNING RESOURCES CENTRE
Havering College
of Further and Higher education

Jessica Kingsley Publishers
London and Philadelphia

First published in 2009
by Jessica Kingsley Publishers
116 Pentonville Road
London N1 9JB, UK
and
400 Market Street, Suite 400
Philadelphia, PA 19106, USA

www.jkp.com

Library of Congress Cataloging in Publication Data
A CIP catalog record for this book is available from the Library of Congress

British Library Cataloguing in Publication Data
A CIP catalogue record for this book is available from the British Library

ISBN 978 1 84905 016 6

Printed and bound in Great Britain by
Athenaeum Press, Gateshead, Tyne and Wear

Contents

Acknowledgements

I owe great thanks to the group members who participated in this project. They shared poignant memories, feelings, and painful moments in their lives, showing such courage and sensitivity. I am deeply appreciative of my relationships with key colleagues including James Holzbauer, Pekka Hanninen, Jamie McMillan, and Paula Turner for providing wonderful company, insights and support, and with whom I have shared more laughs than imaginable. Finally, without David Pitt, our director, the project would never have taken place. David provided unending support throughout and advocated for the funds needed for the supervising psychologist.

I am grateful to my family, including my parents, David and Joan and sisters, Sara and Linda, for their love and ongoing generosity. Both of my parents helped in teaching me how to write, to be disciplined and to strive for whatever I felt I could achieve. My sisters are talented, compassionate and humanitarian in their outlook – their presence is always an inspiration.

Finally, I wish to thank my husband Marc for his patient editing, loving advice and capacity to be a maverick. Marc, through his wisdom and goodness, has quietly taught me that just being is enough.

Preface

This book chronicles the journey of four individuals with developmental disabilities who participated in a group therapy project over many months. This is not a book about promoting group therapy as a viable means to "treat" people with developmental disabilities. Rather, it is a text meant to challenge professionals, family members and community to communicate with those who have a developmental disability using authentic dialogue. While this may sound relatively easy, even trite and ordinary, closer examination of our communication patterns with persons who are developmentally disabled reveals how rarely authentic dialogue is achieved. Although I had worked in the field of developmental disabilities for approximately 15 years at the time of starting the group therapy project, I was shocked and humbled as the poignant tales that each of the group members shared with us dispelled my expectations. I began to realize that my beliefs and impressions were in many respects as prejudicial as the communities that I had worked so hard to educate. I had wrongly assumed that persons with developmental disabilities could not express or acquire the level of emotional insight and sensitivity that was witnessed in our groups. For those who actively advocate for, or directly care for, or provide a service for a distinct group of individuals, the most formidable dangers relate to our own blind spots, not conservative governments or incompetent staff. By blind spots, I am referring to a subconscious and, at times, conscious "seduction" of the difference that we perceive in the person. By that I mean that being disabled dominates the worker or caregiver's vision such that we overcompensate and, generally, lower our expectations of the individual's capabilities. I believe this phenomenon to be the Achilles heel of social work. We pride ourselves as professionals on our ability to recognize difference and then try to forget, even pretend that it is not there so as to claim we are working within a normalizing framework. And yet it is impossible to forget and, ultimately, hurtful. In the process of normalizing all aspects of the developmentally disabled persons' lives, we deny them the dignity of authentic dialogue and relationship.

Ironically, the intensity of effort on the part of professionals to frame or explain a person's circumstances in a way that can be perceived as helpful precludes the fundamental task of determining how to be helpful. For the developmentally disabled most of the professional focus has been to increase levels of independent living with greater exposure to community opportunities. Yet many of the stories that I heard in group therapy were related to themes of fear, anger, and the sense of loss with respect to the disability. Community living for a developmentally disabled person is, at times, a very painful existence, one fraught with loneliness and isolation. Somehow service providers, in their effort to promote equality of opportunity, deny the expanse of emotional trauma that is associated with knowing one's difference. I experienced tremendous resistance and discomfort from colleagues when I described the painful emotions and topics that surfaced within the groups. In fact, one colleague emphatically denied that the developmentally disabled are different and that my case studies should demonstrate how insightful and intuitive they are, as a miracle "Forrest Gump-like" phenomenon. Forrest Gump exuded the child-like innocence that many adults with developmental disabilities are attributed with as a means of side-stepping their adult needs. Forrest Gump was harmless, endearing and exuded only positive emotion that won the hearts of those around him – a caricature of the well-adjusted disabled person. An important element that emerged from the group psychotherapy project has been to reserve *positive* judgment about an individual's character and capabilities in the same way that it is of obvious importance to withhold negative judgment.

Like all of us, developmentally disabled persons carry a mix of emotions, all of which deserve to be acknowledged. Typically, we have ignored the pain of the developmentally disabled by denying the grief they experience at the loss of a "normal" life, a theme that emerged continuously in the group therapy project. Yet, by giving safe and nurturing space to *all* levels of emotion, the developmentally disabled can be afforded the dignity they deserve. It is patronizing and humiliating to be disregarded, not for being different, but for being genuine. Rather than lowering our expectations by adopting child-like voices as we so often do when communicating with the developmentally disabled, we must find the courage to meet the individual face-to-face, one human being to another, not by denying difference but by striving for a deeper level of mutual acceptance. So often we try to hide our feelings of inadequacy in communicating with the developmentally disabled and mask this with authoritarian-style dialogue. Genuine dialogue is the groundwork for establishing the "dignity of risk" that is so often talked about in the field. Usually this refers to something like allowing someone to ride the subway alone or to live in their own apartment. By assuming the dignity of risk in communication, we can free ourselves and allow the other the freedom to be.

Introduction

Surprisingly, at the age of 23, I found myself considering a job working with the mentally retarded – the label developmentally disabled persons were given at that time. Not too many people seek out a career to work with people with developmental disabilities. Marginalized populations and those staff who surround them are all discriminated against. At best, job experience with the developmentally disabled is hoped to be a launching pad for those who wish to do more socially recognized work. Those with developmental disabilities are often seen as never improving and so fall into a system of caretaking rather than one of treatment. This was not something I thought much about at the time of my new job, though I do remember an older colleague had told me not to worry, that I could make lots of "mistakes" helping the retarded without ever having to be concerned about any serious consequences. It was a cold and cruel tenet that was adopted by many in the field. I was not sure exactly what he was referring to until I observed that within agencies for the developmentally disabled there are ultimately few checks and balances, and little accountability. I am not suggesting that emotional and physical abuse was in any way commonplace; on the contrary, I worked with many well-intentioned and dedicated staff. Rather, I am suggesting that the "clients'" emotional needs were given secondary consideration and often deemed unimportant – a tacit understanding amongst administrators who struggled to maintain budgets, please families and ensure staff were reasonably satisfied.

I came from a loving and supportive family, and had a cousin who had Down's syndrome. Every holiday we got together with my cousins and Peter was a prominent member, always included in all of the family functions; he had a great sense of humor and was devoted to all of us. I admired how my parents, sisters, aunt, and cousins treated him with such dignity, with high expectations of both his capacity to develop skills and good relationships. My sisters and I were heartened by his progress, though at times self-conscious about receiving stares from others when he accompanied us in the community. At the interview for my first job with the developmentally disabled I described details about Peter's life and how that somehow made me qualified to work with others like him. Though I was excited about getting hired, I knew at the time that the job would not receive any accolades from my community. It was particularly embarrassing when it was discovered that my salary was so low I could barely afford to drive the car that my parents had generously given me. So the personal sacrifices that were to come over many years really began on my first day in the field of developmental disabilities. At best, my friends hoped it was a stepping stone to something else. Within a few years, I quickly developed ambitions of launching into a more productive kind of social work. I had made up my mind that there was no way I could survive very long in what began to feel like the start of a dead-end career. I had little awareness of how oppressed those with developmental disabilities are and the subsequent effect on the staff who work with them.

My first impressions of the work were a mixture of curious interest about the odd sorts of problems that presented themselves and an uncertainty about how to respond. For example, I encountered one individual who compulsively collected garbage, stockpiling it in her apartment before being evicted. One day, I opened my office door only to find my client, stark naked, staring and laughing at my shocked face. I worked with a woman whose anger became so volatile that she would scream within a few inches of our faces. I became the counselor for a young woman whose aggression required us to restrain and drag her to a time out room on a regular basis. Then there were the more hilarious stories of everyday, ordinary routines such as that of the gentleman whose job it was to cook dinner as one of his life skills programs – he thawed the pork chops by putting them in the dryer.

Not surprisingly, I developed a keen interest in learning what I could about how to modify people's behavior. One of the easiest jobs for me to get in the summer of 1981 was a contract position in which I acquired the job of a "life skills counselor", working with workshop trainees that other staff described as the "highest functioning" at their employment training center. These individuals had the misfortune of knowing they were different and felt ashamed to be associated with their peers, maintaining that they were not disabled; at the same time, they knew they were different from "normal" society. At first, I was impressed with their skills compared to the others in the center and was greatly relieved that I did not have to handle any behavior problems. (Little did I know that the future would "bless" me with a job as a behavior management therapist.) It was my job to teach as many life skills to this elite group as was possible in the space of three months. Having very little of any life experience at the age of 23, I panicked. I hid my anxiety well enough to be complemented by my supervisor, who expressed how remarkably confident I was. I had recently become a vegetarian and believed in exercise and felt my best effort would be in getting my "clients" to eat better and exercise more. I decided to organize the hour of teaching that I had been designated into structured lessons and developed all kinds of forms to document my progress. We covered everything from how to balance a weekly allowance to writing down everything that was eaten in a day. I wasn't sure what this would accomplish except that it provided me with pages of documentation to substantiate why the agency should continue to accept government funding for my job. I did not have enough insight at that time to realize how institutional my behaviors were. They were institutional in the sense that, like staff in closed facilities who were demonized for their practices, I did not have full commitment to community integration; I was looking to mould my clients in whatever way possible to ensure compliance of the rules. Despite the fact that I was employed in workshops and residential homes in the community, the clients had little freedom to express themselves, particularly about the absurdities of the system. None of the other staff I had met, even those in senior positions, were able to explain the concept of integration despite the fact that we spoke about it continuously. Although I prided myself on my willingness to embrace the concept of "normalization" and to train my clients to adopt behaviors that were mainstream, ultimately I was unable either to respond with genuineness or to accept their raw emotions.

When I left that summer job, I felt sad about the lives of two women in particular, both of whom had shared their life's pain with me and their bitterness. They knew how patronized they were and imprisoned within the "integrated" system society had created to ease its conscience and its purse – a system which guarantees an increase of skills *and* loneliness. The institutions were costly and falling out of favor and we, like a rescue squad, were entering these arcane structures to select the lucky person who had been chosen for a transfer to one of our community group homes.

I was as guilty as the administrators for putting aside my feelings about what felt right and desensitizing myself to the rote and predictable ways that we related to our clients. Thus began a long process of dissociation from the emotional pain and loneliness that I experienced in working with the developmentally disabled. I had convinced myself that it was necessary to operate within a cocoon, denying my clients genuine emotional interaction in order to keep from developing what I thought was a condition of burnout, a staff affliction that is rampant in the field of developmental disabilities, one that is considered a reflection of failure. I convinced myself that the summer had been highly successful overall, especially since some of my group members had even started jogging regularly. My supervisor was especially pleased with the way I had been able to manage my job with little input from her. She suffered the plight of most administrative social workers – accountability at the expense of creativity and humane relationships. The workshop was filled with staff who seemed to have lost their spirit and I looked critically on those who were labeled as burned out. Those staff were described as just having been there too long and worked with too many frustrating, problem-behavior clients. I can remember getting stuck in the offices of some of these individuals and hearing them complain about the system, the administration and their lousy paying jobs for what felt like hours of tortuous listening. I naïvely thought that there was a way to inspire them out of their state and that with the right touch I could eventually reach them. I guess what became most disturbing was the way in which I felt the staff were committing a moral offense by giving up on the ones who were really suffering. It took many years before I understood that both staff and client under the rubric of normalization avoided each other's emotional essence. We learned to ignore our clients' emotional pain because it was a disruption to the system, to the skills they were learning, those that we credited with so much importance. It was not intentionally harmful, yet we caused pain. By striving towards the ideal of "normal" we sidestepped genuine connection, denying individuals their identity.

Many of the staff I have encountered throughout my career were people struggling with the same kinds of problems encountered by the individuals we "served". Yet, we as "the staff" desperately tried to differentiate ourselves from those who were deemed to have the disability. The fear of falling under the control of caretakers like ourselves unconsciously played on our decisions to maintain a clear distinction. However, there was great reluctance to honestly face the similarities that connected us all under the flawed normalizing systems that we operated within. It took many years to develop the freedom and even the ability to stand back and understand from a different perspective. I am grateful to the few colleagues who also felt there was something to gain by doing the same. We risked exposing ourselves and our colleagues and offending those in the system with power.

No one had cautioned me about the dangers of adopting institutional behaviors as the community was considered free of such horrors. We were working in the community and it was therefore assumed that institutional attitudes were as far away as the buildings that had previously housed many of the persons we were working with. Any suggestion or reference to the group home or workshop life as being an institutional experience was sacrilege. So my colleagues and I developed institutional patterns of relating to the developmentally disabled without recognizing it, without having to concede. It just happened, it was the norm and easy to adopt. I, like many others, was particularly vulnerable because of a personal mission to establish status and control, both of which are reinforced continuously in North American cultures from an early age. My role models corroborated and praised my good intentions. I worked very hard to control and legitimize sanctified practices and approaches to demonstrate how consistently professional our work setting was. The most valuable and effective tool we were taught was found in the theory and practices of behavior modification. We all took introductory courses on behavior management throughout the 1980s. It was considered vital and also carried with it a sense of accomplishment once one had mastered the principles and programs. Those staff who worked in the houses utilizing behavior modification practices were considered to be among the most skilled, and were even paid more money than the rest of us. Working with a "behavior-challenged" client became the learning ground for behavior theories and practices. We poured out programs, charts, checklists and rewards to turn around those who were "non-compliant". It became an obsession, a means of establishing credibility and success in the field. The behavior programs were a convenient way of establishing accountability and justifying funds for additional supports – it was reinforced at the highest levels of government.

I worked hard to refine my skills as a behavior modifier, reducing my dialogue to brief conversations revolving around "Let's review your schedule," "What should you be doing right now?", or "Why did you do that?" Behavior modification is certainly valuable, however, as the dominant mode of interaction it becomes detrimental. No one is capable of favorable responding when emotional investment is masked, even annihilated. We had charts lining the walls of the office recording behaviors, performance and what were, ultimately, our prideful achievements. We handed out nickels, Smarties, even pieces of cheese as a motivator for those labeled "problematic". The better I got at it, the less reasonable I became. Problems were analyzed, targeted and solved. It was a quick and, often times, an effective way of dealing with complex unsolvable problems that would have meant a declaration of failure on our part. It was during these early years that I felt the most disconnected from myself and others. I did not give up on behavior management for a long, long time. We felt that the never-ending quest for the right reinforcer would eventually alleviate most of our problems. Indeed, solving the problem became a mission, and even more important than the human connection. It was not until we began working with Dr. Wai Yung Lee, a social worker who declared "the emperor has no clothes", that the process of why we felt the need to problem-solve was explored. We began to do role plays in our sessions with Wai Yung to increase the range of emotion in both ourselves and those we were working with. It was a safe place to release the anger, frustration, and even feelings of hatred that we had harbored for a long period of time. As well, role playing highlighted the ridiculousness of many of the situations that were so seriously described. Indeed, we were taking ourselves too seriously in the sense that there was no room for any of us to breathe. What was particularly interesting about the role plays was the ability of the staff to easily adopt the characters of the clients with all kinds of emotional expression and range. To play ourselves, the staff, in a freer and expressive manner was considerably more difficult. There were a number of debates about the value of the role play and whether or not it was worthwhile because after all it was not the real thing. Ironically though, the role plays were uncomfortable because they were *too* real an experience for many of us to handle. The role plays surfaced layers of repressed and unconscious desires that could not be acted upon for fear of losing one's job. In the safety of Wai Yung's training, these desires could be faced and reckoned with as a means of establishing an authenticity we had previously avoided.

Many years went by before we established the group therapy project. And while we had been consistently working on honest and "real" feedback up until the project began, we were still reticent to relinquish degrees of power and control. It was astounding how powerfully these needs dominated our professional roles and those of our staff. The group therapy would prove to be an exciting forum with which to develop our skills and our character even further. Most importantly, we would learn to sit side-by-side, staff and client, in genuine dialogue. We were ready to test ourselves, to tease apart the walls of separation, to meet each other's eyes in recognition of our universal psyche.

The use of group psychotherapy for the developmentally disabled population raises the question as to whether or not any group of people who collectively distinguish themselves from the general population need to be "treated". Certainly, many of the emotional difficulties that developmentally disabled persons experience have been attributed to their marginalized position in society. As a result, great efforts have been made on the part of service providers to ensure that integration into society affords the developmentally disabled as many of the benefits as any "normal" individual might experience. Indeed, the principle of normalization has been expounded and developed within the field for decades, providing a framework for agencies to apply integration in such a way as to restore normal living. However, I believe that many developmentally disabled persons would benefit from a therapeutic environment because *they* perceive their differences, regardless of how their service providers view them. In the effort to advocate for the rights of the disabled, we often overlook their emotional pain – the pain of being stigmatized and knowing that one's disability is permanent. Persons with developmental disabilities can tell when others look down on them, they are hurt emotionally when people ridicule them, and they realize that their opportunities are restricted because others view them as incapable. Additionally, many persons with developmental disabilities suffer from an inordinately high number of psychiatric disorders and dramatic life events that justify the need for therapeutic services specific to their circumstances.

The developmentally disabled have traditionally been viewed as not capable of responding to psychodynamic treatment; there is a general cultural attitude that correlates intelligence with a challenging and responsive "client". While developmentally disabled persons have been the subject of numerous research studies in the field of behavior therapy, with some positive outcomes, the impetus to apply and research cognitive-based therapies has been minimal with this population. Not only have the developmentally disabled suffered from segregation by being forced to live in institutions, they have also been segregated within the psychotherapeutic community by being ignored. Psychotherapists have had a tendency to view the developmentally disabled in the same way that non-professionals view this population – as uninteresting and unattractive. Often, the presence of emotional disturbances is attributed to the developmental lag and not treated as it would be in the normal population, despite the fact that the symptoms for both populations are the same. In addition, for persons who are developmentally disabled a distinction is made between the practice of counseling, which is considered necessary, and psychotherapy, which is viewed as unnecessary. In fact, the majority of staff positions held in group homes or institutions have the title "counselor" inserted. Counseling, as it is used in this context, is considered to mean the application of direction and practical assistance to solving living-situational problems, or to developing social skills. In contrast, psychotherapy focuses on changing aspects of an individual's personality that causes them problems in managing daily living and a subjective sense of self. Many parents and professionals view psychotherapy with unrealistic and archaic attitudes of madness or mystery. Counseling for the developmentally disabled is even regarded as an inferior form of practice and consequently they are viewed with an exaggerated pessimism and ignorance. They have also been regarded as too unintelligent to recognize the significant negative social conditions which they encounter daily, such as stigmatization, loneliness, and unemployment, to name a few.

A high percentage of persons with developmental disabilities also suffer from psychiatric illnesses and the trauma of sexual abuse. It is important to note that even those individuals who may not suffer from trauma may still require supportive interventions to cope with the stress that an awareness of difference creates. Specifically, a number of negative social conditions that many persons with developmental disabilities encounter include: being labeled, being rejected and ridiculed, segregation, being infantilized – the tendency to be treated like a child, a high degree of social disruption that occurs as a result of movement from one facility to another and the high rates of turnover of other residents and staff, and restricted opportunities as it relates to finding meaningful employment. In the effort to apply the theory of normalization and counteract the pernicious effects of institutionalization in previous decades, many professionals have overlooked the tremendous stresses that developmentally disabled people must face in community living. Like any one of us, persons with developmental disabilities who struggle to contend with the above negative social conditions may experience extreme emotional difficulty during these crisis times. Often the person is not attributed with the ability to cope with feelings and therefore caregivers and family may deny their grief or sadness, which ultimately leads to increased suppression of these emotions and prolonged pain. We witnessed this over and over during the group project, and had to finally admit that we had not believed group members were capable of the depth of feeling that emerged.

There are predictable crises in the lives of developmentally disabled people due to the convergence of emotional stresses at significant times in their lives such as: the birth of siblings, starting school, puberty in adolescence, being surpassed by younger siblings, the departure of siblings, the end of education, leaving the parental home, illness and death of parents, and death of peers or loss of friends. Often, the person is not attributed with the ability to cope with feelings during these formative periods. It can also be argued that the developmentally disabled are at risk of acquiring mental illnesses because of a lack of support for the many emotional stresses that they experience. Emotional disturbance can develop as an outcome of being denied one's feelings whether that be rejection, lack of self-worth, or the fear of having to develop greater independence, tied to the fear of separation.

One of our chief concerns in selecting individuals for the group therapy project was whether or not the person was articulate enough to participate. This inevitably led to a discussion as to whether or not the group member was of a functioning level high enough to have insight, be concerned about their ability to adjust and communicate verbally. My staff and I had all taught a number of groups focusing on teaching assertiveness skills and life skills. Although we had spent many years in various professional settings from group homes to vocational workshops, we had never considered running a group based on the exploration of emotional issues and personality. We had to rethink our criteria for group therapy and realized that it should expand beyond the factor of intelligence and, rather, include motivation for change. Therapeutic-based groups have been regarded, even among advocates for the developmentally disabled, as only suitable for higher functioning individuals. We also had to give up the idea of using behavior management strategies within the groups and refrain from a reward–punishment modality. We wanted the dynamic to be spontaneous, heartfelt, and genuine rather than a role play responding to what might be deemed as "correct" social interaction. The reported success of our group project may be related to the fact that global concepts and not specific behaviors were measured, thereby enhancing more complex dynamics that were required to maintain successful social interaction. We wanted to avoid a simplistic model and frames of social interaction as a series of "right" and "wrong" answers. Essentially, the groups were run in such a way as to critically examine whether group therapy was a viable means of helping individuals learn to cope with their stigmatized identity. Some of the more interesting findings included the difficulty members had in acknowledging their disabilities, as witnessed by the refusal to speak about it, or not remembering being called or treated as disabled – hence a denial of self. There was a tendency by some to refer to the phenomenon of stigmatization by dissociating their emotions from the language used to describe their label. For example, one man spoke about himself in a language that was devoid of any reference to a disability. Many of the groups eventually developed the trust and comfort to talk about daily experiences and how the impact of being disabled continued to affect them. They also achieved the ability to describe in their own language the manifestations of being disabled, including emotional distress or other difficulties restricting independence, such as the ability to handle money. Finally, group members eventually responded with some dialogue of self-acceptance and acceptance of others in spite of the stigmatization. There were many examples of group members coming to recognize each other as people they could derive support from and to whom their care and advice would be regarded as valuable. They were also able to show compassion and understanding for group members who were clearly struggling, rather than using the presence of others for downward comparison.

As leaders, we employed counseling techniques in such a way as to permit and encourage the participants to express whatever thoughts and feelings came to mind. Many of the prominent themes that emerged in the groups were: independence, romantic relationships, sense of self-worth, loneliness, dreams of self-encouragement, and support by family members. We employed counseling techniques framed in a non-directed milieu with the explicit purpose of accepting and attending to whatever the group members' chose. We also adopted a phenomenological orientation, one which set aside theories and preconceptions, in order to determine what the understanding of the personal worlds of developmentally disabled adults encompasses without bias, in their language. Thus, the groups were unique in presenting the personal perspectives of the developmentally disabled in a group therapy forum in which there was considerable effort to proceed with an unbiased agenda or goal. The phenomenological approach seemed especially appropriate for understanding the personal worlds of developmentally disabled adults who are rarely asked to share their perspectives or credited with the validity of their experiences. Frequency of participation, group cohesiveness, and the sharing of deep personal feelings with displays of emotion were all observed to increase over the three to four months during which the groups were held.

Emotional connection provides a valuable approach in meeting the mental health needs of persons with developmental disabilities, as well as being a useful means of establishing ongoing support during particularly difficult life experiences. The advantages of group therapy are many: sharing information and experiences, peer and therapist modeling, confrontation, group support and encouragement, problem-solving, cohesion, and efficient use of resources. By sharing information about life experiences, individuals who have been isolated or are uncertain of themselves can increase their skills and build confidence as they gain knowledge from their peers and therapists. Topics may be covered that group members would otherwise have been afraid to ask about or disclose, in particular with peers. Group therapy is but one of a number of viable means of reducing the negative emotions that may be associated with particular subjects by revealing the universality of suffering. Inextricably linked to group discussion is the phenomenon of modeling, which also provides a medium for adapting new attitudes and skills by observing someone who is more capable than us in a specific area of development. The skill of confrontation which includes both the ability to confront another as well as the opportunity to express ideas and emotions can flourish in a group process. Group work also facilitates learning to establish one's identity and refine the ability to recognize emotions, both one's own and those of group members. For many persons with developmental disabilities there is a tendency to be unassertive due to dependency on others and low self-esteem, both of which result in poor confrontation skills. We were surprised and delighted to observe group members rise to the occasion and use confrontation in positive ways. It should also be said that we observed some of the more devastating results of confrontation when used to malign others. As staff, we resisted the temptation to take over the situation, rather we respected the rights of those individuals who were marginalized to speak for themselves.

Peer support and encouragement is extremely important for the developmentally disabled as so many individuals perceive themselves as failures and suffer from terrible isolation. Hence, the ability to form and maintain relationships is paramount considering their dependency on others, and the stigmatization they may suffer due to the presence of maladapted behaviors. Problem-solving does not necessarily mean finding the answer on how to handle specific situations, rather there may be a personality trait, a "blind spot", that is preventing relationships from succeeding; feedback from peers and a therapist can be pivotal in both the perception and motivational responses needed to change specific behaviors. Often, persons with developmental disabilities are starved for a cohesive belonging in any group, yet may shun association with other disabled persons due to prejudicial attitudes. One of the essential components of group therapy is the development and maintenance of group cohesiveness – the process of sharing oneself and receiving acceptance by others. It is acceptance that we all starve for, despite whatever repugnant, unacceptable perceptions we internalize and come to believe that we possess. Essentially, the power behind group therapy is the creation of opportunity to be emotionally supported at vulnerable moments, those we fear can never be revealed.

In addition to treating mental illness, or supporting victims of sexual abuse, or those in relapse prevention, genuine dialogue can be applied as a means to bolster an individual through the many difficulties of life. Many professionals, in their desire to uphold the notion that establishing a normal lifestyle and integration in the community is paramount, have side-stepped the emotional needs of the developmentally disabled for fear of having to admit their differences and thus appearing to be unprofessional. Many workers have a tendency to speak to persons with developmental disabilities with an intonation not unlike that of a teacher to a child. They also feel the need to erase negative reactions, to assume a perpetually positive expression and over-emphasize positive praise. And for the client, the pressure to maintain a positive and well-adjusted appearance is just one more mask individuals struggle to hide behind in order to ensure a positive response from family, caregivers, and peers. It is clear that many developmentally disabled persons are acutely aware of their differences and suffer tremendous emotional strife as a result of being denied a normal life; this is not a phenomenon related to mental illness and does not need to be "treated" as such, but it does need to be acknowledged. It is my belief that many of the developmentally disabled individuals who are aware of their loss and limitations silently suffer as they strive to deny those feelings. Emotional development with persons who are developmentally disabled is so often ignored or reduced to simplistic descriptions and discounted despite its importance in attaining their happiness. We are outraged by the institutions that have imprisoned persons with developmental disabilities and yet, unwittingly, imprison them by denying who they are. The more attention we can give to the emotional dimensions of being developmentally disabled, the more we will appreciate the humanity of developmentally disabled people. This increased sensitivity could have a positive influence on the way we react to developmentally disabled persons, how our agencies are organized and how our policies are developed.

By genuinely focusing on the needs of the whole person, rather than putting all our effort into erasing the developmental deficit, we approach normalcy on a dimension generally deemed to be impossible to attain. Indeed, the individuals that participated in the group therapy project taught us acceptance, forgiveness, how to withhold judgment, and to develop the strength to be vulnerable. The project endured over the course of approximately 12 weeks with each group session lasting one hour. We interviewed each individual who showed interest in the project, explaining what was entailed, discussing issues of confidentiality, and outlining the level of discussion that might occur. Once the 12 weeks were finished, we followed up with each group member, using an interview format, and gave them the opportunity to provide feedback on the value of the experience. It should also be noted that we always allowed the designated staff of each group member to participate in the initial and follow-up interview. On occasion we also met with family members but only at the request of a group member. Because the project forged new ground we felt it was important to stay well connected and give each other as much feedback as possible. As a result, each of us assumed the role of an 'observer' in groups that we were not leading by sitting in the back of the room and taking notes, or pensively gathering observations for post-session. This observation process allowed us to grasp the experience 'live'; and like good theatre, we, the audience, became part of the drama that ensued. We also decided to employ a supervising psychologist, Dr. Shapero, whose area of expertise was group therapy. He was invited to sit in, like the observers, once a week for each group that was running. By doing it this way he and the observers had firsthand knowledge of the sessions and a unique perspective that would have been difficult to acquire by listening to an audiotape or reviewing a video. Surprisingly, due to the intensity of the experience and the immense concentration that was required, the observers and Dr. Shapero's presence posed little source of performance anxiety. And at times, it was comforting to be surrounded by colleagues who were so committed. Before long, there were many curious onlookers as the group members filed into the room where the sessions took place and we often heard how the group members spoke about their experiences with such pride. We all felt that our participation was creating experiences that we would carry for many years.

Patricia – Standing Tall

Patricia's relaxed and comfortable style in the interview was unusual relative to the others. Part of our selection process for new members was to arrange an interview in which we explained what the groups were all about, as well as to give us a chance to determine someone's suitability for participation. She remarked "cool" to most of my descriptions about group therapy and what she might look forward to experiencing. Having just come back from a trip in Utah, I had heard a lot of that particular word (a southwest favorite), so I smiled at Patricia and asked her if she was also a frequent user of "awesome". She had a good sense of humor and enjoyed our jocular exchange. Towards the end of the interview she surprised me when on a much more serious note she exclaimed "I want to learn to stand tall like my sister and to be outspoken. I may have Down's syndrome, but I'm smart." Patricia seemed somewhat taken aback by her own frankness and said "I never talk about these things." We were impressed that she felt comfortable to be so honest and I quickly felt an affinity with and fondness for her.

I did not expect Patricia's behavior to play out in the scripted way that it did for the first three sessions; she would come about 15 minutes late and then fall asleep or withdraw for the first 25 minutes. When addressed by either myself or Marco, the other group leader, she seemed willing to participate and generally contributed in a meaningful way. However, if our attention turned to someone else in the group, Patricia drifted off. I was not sure if she needed to be the star, or if her adjustment to the process was self-protection – to appear only mildly invested.

Marco and I realized that we were beginning to afford Patricia a deference that the other group members did not receive. We had not addressed her sleeping, her lateness, or her aloofness. We both agreed that her presence in the group was important to us and that we had a fear of losing her, perhaps because her Adult Protective Service Worker had said to me "I didn't refer Patricia to the group because she tends to be a no-show." We felt then that there was some accomplishment in the fact that she was attending at all and were reluctant to push her.

There was another important pattern that we identified within the first three weeks relating to Patricia's behavior. One of the other women in the group knew her through various other social contacts and was clearly mesmerized by her. Mary watched Patricia carefully in the sessions, and tried to engage her in whatever capacity she could, even if it meant irritating Patricia by speaking for her, interrupting, or making constant reference to the past. Patricia's response was often to smile at Mary, nod her head and put up her hand as if to say "enough of that". In spite of the outward positive affect, it was clear that Mary was an irritant at times and we helped facilitate a discussion between them in which Patricia could tell Mary how she was feeling. While that was somewhat helpful, I felt it remained fairly superficial and that there were all kinds of other feelings being exchanged, although they were not clear to me at the time.

It was not until Marco and I had a very difficult time with one session dealing with the topic of attractions that we began to consider the possibility that Mary was physically attracted to Patricia, and that neither of them necessarily knew. Marco and I had strongly disagreed with each other after the session ended and were both quite angry about the other's interpretation of what went wrong. I felt we were both responsible in pursuing a topic that was far too threatening and risky for the group's third session. Perhaps the good that came out of it was the challenge from one of the observers and leaders of another group that we were treading on dangerous ground. What if Mary had strong sexual feelings for Patricia? We might have forced her into a frightening and embarrassing position by our insinuation that attraction between the men and women in the group be openly declared (although that was not at all the goal we were after).

Patricia proved to be a valuable member of the group when in session four one of the men made an off-handed joke. She clearly identified his anger towards her and felt the need to both pursue his feelings and to help him overcome these emotions. It seemed as though Patricia had taken the feedback from the previous week, that she come on time, stay awake, and participate in a more active way, to heart. Her commitment to the problem the group was struggling with, to help Carl deal with his anger, was clearly present.

It was not until the fifth week that Patricia brought up her original goal of "standing tall". It seemed as though the other members knew what she was referring to, although she did not equate it with her developmental disability. For some reason I lost my nerve and chose not to bring up the pain of being disabled as it related to her comments. I also remembered how difficult it was to broach this topic with the first group I worked with six months previously. It seems strange that as professionals we are so reticent and fearful of open discussion on the topic of disability with those who clearly feel the affliction of the handicap most significantly. In spite of the fact that Mary talked about her learning disability at the beginning of the group, neither Marco nor myself helped them to discuss this important topic. We kept pressuring Patricia to explain herself further and describe the meaning behind this not so cryptic phrase of "standing tall." Patricia was clearly uncomfortable by the end of the session for having raised a topic that even the group leaders were struggling with. She closed with: "I know everyone is cool, I don't want to bring anyone down."

"I would have preferred the topic of 'standing tall' rather than death," was the feedback we received from Dr. Shapero at the end of the next session. Marco and I were both somewhat embarrassed and baffled when we realized that we had again skirted away from the topic. The group had started out in a very disjointed manner and Adam, who usually contributed in a very meaningful way, was clearly fading on us from the moment we began. I pursued a line of questioning with him that had more to do with his physical ailment (Adam was suffering from muscular dystrophy), rather than his emotional state. Even though Adam clearly indicated that he was not himself, and was feeling quite a bit of frustration, I continued to project my interpretation of what I had heard. I had missed one of Yalom's cardinal axioms: pay attention to the here-and-now and respond to what you see, not just to what you hear. I felt particularly bad for Patricia at the end of the session once I realized where we had gone wrong. For the second week in a row, the leaders avoided the topic that was most pressing. I wondered if she was asking herself whether we had the guts to deal with it. Even though we covered everything from physical pain to death, the discussion did not seem to lead to much bonding. I felt that we had still not achieved the level of intimacy with Patricia that she was hoping for. Although she responded with some comments on the topic of death, it seemed that she was doing so to show some active participation in the group and not because she was emotionally invested.

One of the most profound and intense exchanges that I had yet to observe was prompted by Patricia's absence at the seventh session. The session had gone quite well from the beginning and I was pleased with the level of detail and openness that had been expressed yet again on the topic of death. This time, we dealt with the death of our parents, a concern and fear that hit close to home for me. Both of my parents suffered from heart disease, most recently my mother, and their inevitable demise seemed to be a reality that I could no longer escape thinking about or preparing for. When Mary admitted to calling her mother every day just to see if she was alive, I identified with her and told her some of my fears. It felt good to share my own feelings, a practice that I had not done much of, having been spurred on by Yalom's writings. Dr. Shapero once described a story to us about a fellow therapist who confessed that he rarely had anyone admit to anger in his group. He then advised his colleague that perhaps it was because he did not allow it. That story had great impact on me and I thought that, not being a very open person, I might unknowingly be inhibiting my groups to retain their feelings.

As the discussion on families, death, and being bossed around drew to a close, I decided to draw attention to the empty chair that would have been Patricia's. The chair became alive when Adam intervened and brought Patricia back into the minds of the group. I was not sure what he was alluding to when he said "I'm confused now, something's really wrong here." I surmised that it had to do with the dialogue two of the women were having that was confusing, except that he said it with such intensity and gravity, that there seemed to be more. He turned to Mary: "If Patricia was sitting in this empty chair, what would you say?" My heart began to pound as I intently focused on Mary; I was shocked by Adam's insight and fascinated that he had intuitively understood her attraction for Patricia. She held her head in one hand, smiled and said flippantly: "I'd say hi. I'll see you later at floor hockey tonight." Adam continued his challenge. "No, she wouldn't say much to that if she were here. She'd be annoyed by that." He had me anxiously waiting for what was next to come. "I think there's something confusing, something wrong." I quietly asked him if he had seen this pattern before between Mary and Patricia. Adam skillfully replied: "Patricia's holding back," to which Marco added: "Is Mary holding back?" Throughout this dialogue the intensity had built to such a point, I was not sure I would be able to stay in my seat. I was spellbound by his dramatic ability to explore the relationship between Patricia and Mary with such proficiency. Adam continued: "Mary is holding back something big in her heart." I asked him if it was easier to say these things in Patricia's absence, to which he replied: "No, I would ask her as well, 'What are you holding back Patricia?' I would want to know what she's thinking. Maybe she doesn't want to talk about things. But she's holding back something. What's the deal?"

I thought I detected a collective sigh of relief when Marco declared the time was almost up; it appeared that any more dialogue at that level of intensity might be overwhelming. Patricia's absence clearly had great impact on everyone and, before departing, they all lamented her disappearance and hoped she would be back next week. Mary said nothing and quietly left.

For most of us working with persons with developmental disabilities, we assume and often hope that our clients will also be sexually delayed. This assumption is held by a good majority of the parents and, surprisingly, many of the administrators of agencies for the developmentally disabled. Many of the odd behaviors exhibited of a sexual nature were just too embarrassing to talk about, and were therefore often tolerated or ignored. As the staff of group homes and workshops received very little support or information on this topic, they relied on a reward–punishment model to cope. Behavior modification tactics could be applied to just about anything, although sexual acting-out behaviors were particularly hard to squelch. Spontaneity with respect to sexual inappropriateness was never considered a solution. Many of us were unable to be spontaneous within the context of our work environments and, interestingly, found that we had to learn to allow ourselves the freedom to be so, to move away from "professional" script that was dull and lifeless.

I learned that vigilance would be critical to good therapy when after our next session, Dr. Shapero said with some frustration: "They didn't get their money's worth today." Marco and I had been so intrigued by Adam's ploy with Patricia, that we failed to respond in a beneficial way to the rest of the group the following week; instead, we were too fascinated with the content of the session, as though we ourselves were participating as group members.

All eyes had been on Patricia when she arrived, and Carl, who usually waited quite some time before speaking, smiled broadly and said "We missed you last week." Then the others joined in with their declarations of loss at Patricia's absence, and once again the intensity started to quickly build around her – this time it was her presence. But what surprised me was Adam's sudden disclosure of deep feelings for Patricia, and his descriptive account of how he feared that something terrible had happened to her. Patricia seemed as confused as I did, exclaiming "I didn't think he cared so much about me." There was a considerable amount of tension as they exchanged words about whether or not this was just a concern or an overture of deeper feelings of attraction. I did not frame their obvious sexual tension as a natural outcome of the type of intimacy that can develop in group therapy, and instead went on to probe Patricia's feelings about her centrality. My attention fed into the grandiosity that Patricia began to feel about herself and the power that Adam attributed to her presence. She declared with some resignation: "Without me, you guys are all breaking apart. I'm like the leader. You guys are way back behind me." Adam quickly reinforced her thinking: "Without her, there's nothing to talk about. Never." Marco jumped in: "How is she so important?" Anthony continued: "She's not shy. She laughs, she says much of importance to this group." Then Sara jumped in: "I missed it when she didn't come last week." I weakly protested Adam's determination to present the group as hopeless without Patricia; it took quite a bit of self-reflection and dialogue with Marco to realize that our responses, or lack thereof, were the result of our own fascination with her as the main protagonist. We had to admit that once again we had deferred to her and this time, it was detrimental to the group. Other members looked subdued and almost forlorn as they mused over their lack of importance – how could we have been so insensitive, so caught up with Patricia's story that we essentially lost sight of everyone else in the room? Our superficiality may have explained why the discussion in the group never penetrated the deeper feelings of attraction or competitiveness that must have been there. Although Mary confessed with some reticence that she was glad to see Patricia, we never invited her to talk about those feelings – we failed to return to Adam's empty chair skit. And even though I eventually permitted the group to move on to another topic, it seemed that many of us were still consumed with Patricia's presence.

Other attractions started to spring up on a more overt level after the group reluctantly stopped staring at Patricia. Carl flirted with Betty under the guise of encouraging her to speak to him so she could overcome her shyness. He was beaming when he turned to her and said: "Were you going to say something? I'm your friend, you can talk to me. Go ahead. How are you doing?" I could not help but think of the 1970s film *Harold and Maude*, as Betty was at least 30 years older than Carl and this was not the first time that their attraction for one another had surfaced. The mix of sexual feelings, or strong attraction and bonding between Betty and Carl, Mary and Patricia, Carl and Adam, and other pairings contributed to complex undertows that I was often swept away by. My concentration and skill was challenged to a greater degree in this group than any other – somehow I kept failing to keep my head above water, and resist the temptation to watch what was going on, rather than direct. I had to accept Dr. Shapero's feedback – Marco and I had both been undisciplined.

We waited almost ten minutes before starting, disappointed and concerned that we would have no chance to redeem ourselves, as only half of the group was sitting in front of us the next week. I had all sorts of worries about the lack of attendance. Had we driven off the others because we agreed with Adam that Patricia was all the mattered? Or perhaps Mary was terrified that we might explore the feelings of the empty chair again. I harbored deep fears that the group might disintegrate at any time with no explanation, due to our own failings as leaders. Consequently, I opened with: "It feels awfully empty today." I continued, trying to mask my disappointment, hoping that we could still accomplish something worthwhile in the session: "Well, it's still a chance to talk. Why don't those of you who are here take advantage of the opportunity for more 'floor' time." Nobody seemed interested. On the contrary, the whole group began to focus on Adam who was visibly sulking because Marco had asked Carl and Adam to sit apart from each other. We had discussed this in detail prior to the session and thought that it might be beneficial to both of them to try a new seating arrangement. Carl was often overshadowed by Adam, and the two whispered to each other constantly, making it quite distracting to others. But Adam would have no part of the separation, or at least was refusing to try it graciously. When Marco and I tried to approach Adam with his feelings, he responded by looking at the floor, his whole body slumped forward, and muttered: "It won't work." As we attempted to elicit from both Adam and Carl their feelings of anger or disappointment, or whatever else was going on (I really was not sure and was surprised by the severity of Adam's reaction), the others began to slowly drift in, first David, then Mary and, finally, Patricia.

But before Patricia had arrived, I decided to move the discussion away from Adam and Carl, and instead talked about the strong loyalties in the group, determined that in this session Marco and I would expose the bond between Mary and Patricia to a more comfortable honesty. I began with: "It's natural that in groups we develop strong feelings for others. I've certainly noticed a number of bonds amongst those of us here." Mary responded by stating that she missed Patricia and wondered where she was. I gently added: "I've noticed a strong bond between you and Patricia, it would be helpful for you to talk about it." Upon reflection later, this was a very frustrating moment for me – if only Mary could just admit to *any* feelings at all, then maybe we could move on. But Mary was not going to let down her guard yet and responded predictably with: "I'll see her at cooking class." At the same time that Mary was blocking her feelings about Patricia, Adam withdrew even further. I decided to declare openly that the group was "stuck", hoping that if they sensed my frustration, something or someone might eventually give.

When Patricia arrived after about 20 minutes, she appeared quite self-conscious, as though anticipating all heads to turn in her direction. I tried to ignore her and continued my discussion with Sara, one of the women who often said very little, on why it was so hard for her to stay on topic. But I found my gaze drifting over in Patricia's direction. She looked nervous and had turned her chair so that she was sitting at an angle. I wondered if she was worried that we were going to admonish her for being late, or if the group would once again turn all their attention to her earlier absence.

Surprisingly, Patricia placed herself in the spotlight when she said to Sara: "When I'm not here you're focused, and when I'm here, you're not so focused." Marco decided to be more direct with Patricia about whether or not her presence strongly determined the other's behavior: "Adam made a comment last week that you're the reason for the group, that without you, there is no group. Is that how you see it?" Surprisingly, Patricia quickly said "Yes." Marco then turned to the others: "What does everyone think, is Patricia the most important?" Betty looked slightly annoyed and with a defiance in her voice immediately said "No," while Mary simultaneously replied "Yes." Then Betty in an unassuming way added that she thought Mary was the most important member. I jumped in to clarify what I thought was going on: "Some of us take a leadership role and others of us hold back more. Each of us we may feel a bond with someone else here or several others here, and in that sense someone may be more important to us individually. In the eyes of the leader, for Marco and I, everyone here is of equal importance." I meant it quite sincerely, but wondered if it was really true. After all, we had faltered badly the previous week because of our fascination with both Adam and Patricia – I only hoped that I succeeded in providing adequate reassurance to the others.

We decided that the moment had finally come for Mary and Patricia and that re-involving Adam might be the best way to approach their feelings. I reminded Adam of his empty chair "technique" and asked him if he could try it again with both women, now that they were present. It was the first time since the group began that he sat upright in his chair, his voice became audible and he looked engaged. "Mary, let's say Patricia is not in her chair, what would you say?" Mary grinned and responded nervously: "I'd think something had happened, that she'd been hit by a car." Anthony added: "Maybe kidnapped?" Mary replied: "Maybe." Patricia blurted out: "I don't know what to do with her!" I asked her what she meant, was it that she did not know what to do with Mary's feelings for her. Patricia replied: "It's something hard to describe." The two women continued to fantasize about how it might be if Patricia was dead, but Mary still could not declare her feelings, even after we all persisted with questions, gentle suggestions, and pleas. Finally, Marco said it for her: "Mary, you appear to have intense feelings for Patricia. It looks special to me. Is that right?" As Mary let out her "Yes," Adam, Patricia, Marco, and myself all visibly gasped with relief and sat back in our chairs. Mary smiled when I asked her if she felt better to have acknowledged it, quietly replying "Yes." Adam added: "Let's take a breather. I'm glad that's over with."

Interestingly, both Patricia and Adam were absent at the next session and the group proved their importance to the leaders and to each other by engaging in a very meaningful discussion about loneliness. Paul, the shyest member of the group, unfolded his innermost fears of being left alone when his parents are gone and how terribly lonely he would feel. The others all nodded with understanding, sharing their own stories and offering to con-cretely support one another by meeting outside of the group. I was pleased for the group and for Patricia; after all, she had felt the weight of the group's needs and if in her absence, they could grow, I expected that she would feel relieved.

However, the next week, Patricia was not so relieved that her importance in the group had shifted from star to a member whose absence and lateness was becoming a problem. The group was continuing to grow in complexity as the dyads of relationships heightened in intensity. Carl and Adam danced in a different way from the previous sessions – they no longer sat together, they expressed their disappointments more openly and their feelings for each other appeared to have deepened. Patricia noticed this and criticized Carl for being too worried about his "image"; she repeated this word several times, although none of us were really clear on exactly what she meant. Patricia then responded with a comment that revealed how concerned she was about her own image: "There's something inside your soul that makes you per-fect even though we're not really perfect." Regretfully, I did not link this thought to the theme that seemed to plague Patricia from the beginning – the struggle to be normal, to learn to stand tall.

She elaborated with more: "I'm not that perfect to the world. I try to be perfect for myself, like when I brush my hair I feel OK." But when asked how she was feeling in the group, Patricia began to back down: "I'm fine" she said with resoluteness. As so often happened, Adam, who had been listening carefully, offered a valid insight: "She's not sure or she's confused about her feelings." I tried to pursue this further by pointing out to Patricia that she still had not offered an explanation for her absence, hoping to punctuate how important her image in the group was to her. Both Marco and I tried a few angles but with no luck. As the pressure intensified on Patricia to account for her absence, she diverted us to Mary: "I noticed you talking about me to be on time, Mary." It was not true, Mary had said nothing for most of the group. I responded: "Why did you include Mary when I asked you a question about where you were last week?" Patricia tried to avoid the obvious and for the first time since the group began, I persistently tried to unravel some of her feelings: "But what did it have to do with Mary?" Patricia replied: "Mary is always worried about me, that Mary!" I had never seen Mary challenge Patricia up until that moment; she seemed slightly irritated when she said: "It's not just me, Sara was also worried." Marco jumped in: "The question remains, why did you choose to talk to Mary instead of the group?" Patricia calmly explained: "She thinks I'm famous." It all began to make sense, Patricia's need for self-importance in the group's eyes and especially to Mary. The attention had been a mix of feeling self-conscious and self-important. Again, Mary disagreed, and this time more strongly, with Patricia: "I don't think you're famous, I just wondered if you were sick last week."

Marco continued to address Patricia's patterns of relating in the group by pointing out that her concern for Mary excluded others, particularly Betty. While Patricia was reluctant to share her real feelings about Mary, she was less reluctant to expose her difficulty with Betty: "I don't know how to say this, it feels like I'm talking to my parents." She paused and elaborated further: "You remind me of my grandmother." Betty usually waited quite some time before responding, but not this time: "In what way?" Patricia replied with measured consideration: "Your clothes. And you both have curly hair." She graciously apologized after noticing Betty's expression of hurt: "Sorry I offended you. Are you angry about me saying that you reminded me of my grandmother?" Betty reluctantly admitted to some anger. It was interesting to observe Patricia addressing the theme of self-image with another group member, knowing how important it was to her, and to all of us.

The last session before the Christmas break was quite significant for Patricia as it was the first time that I had chastised her with some intensity – an attempt that was a bit clumsy on my part. Betty opened with: "Patricia isn't here." I found it irritating as Patricia's lateness was becoming routine and it robbed the group's attention until she arrived. We were pursuing Adam and Carl's obvious change of seating (they no longer sat next to each other) when, after about 20 minutes had gone by, Patricia nervously entered the room, sat down with her chair askew and averted her gaze from the group. I decided not to address her right away and continued my discussion with the two men. We were finishing up an important point about how difficult it was for them to talk honestly about how they were really feeling when I turned to Patricia: "I can't help but notice that you've turned your chair sideways." She replied: "I saw you guys were talking." I continued: "You came in late, almost 20 minutes, in spite of our talking about it last week. It's disappointing." Both Carl and Adam expressed their disappointment and when Patricia explained that she had been at a Christmas party, I detected some irritation in her voice. When I asked her about it, she replied: "It reminds me of my parents. I do want to fix it, but it's hard." Carl seemed offended and quickly responded: "We're not your parents." We all started in with another round of protestation: "Can you try to come in earlier?", "You've had reasons for being late, maybe you're not that interested in the group. What are your reasons?", "We wonder about your commitment." Patricia was probably feeling overwhelmed and replied meekly: "I know." We persisted: "Is it OK to be late with other friends outside of the group?", "You weren't thinking that you'd hear from the group the way you do from your parents?" Patricia seemed to be sinking further back: "I feel cornered. Everyone is staring." I tried to reassure her that getting feedback is an uncomfortable process but I knew that Patricia and I were not connecting and that she probably felt isolated by the experience. I regretted that we had ended with such ambivalence before our two-week break and thought about Patricia more than once over the holidays – I did not expect to see her back.

Much to my surprise, Patricia was there at the next session in January and right on time. In fact she was seated in her chair before I was. It proved to be an important session for her, as it was one of the few times that she shared her feelings about a painful event in her life. Sara burst into tears when she relayed that her uncle had died during the holidays, and so began the topic of death. As Sara told the details of the whole event, Patricia's head slowly dropped and I thought for a moment that she had fallen asleep. When Mary asked her if she was tired, she replied: "I can't believe what you are talking about." Marco pursued Patricia to determine if she had also experienced grief. I was not expecting to hear anything from her as we had talked about other deaths in the group before, particularly parents, and she had never referred to anyone close to her as having died. So when she began to tell us the story of the death of her camp director, a "good friend", I listened intently: "In the winter, long ago, my good friend died. I knew her a long time. I have pictures too. She died after a crash coming back from Guelph. There was black ice, a truck turned around and hit the car." She did not say much more after that, although when asked if it was helpful to talk about it, she quietly agreed. It was a short piece between Patricia and the group, but a significant one. We had all related to her as the leader, someone who showed little vulnerability and I was relieved that, as a first step, we saw the frightened and frail side of Patricia. I wondered how comfortable she was really feeling.

Patricia was absent the following week and for the first time Mary expressed her disappointment and frustration with her disappearing acts, as did the majority of the group. Carl started first: "She should call." Then Mary began: "She wasn't in cooking class either. When she's here she falls asleep. You've seen Patricia nod off." Marco then asked the group what was the worst part for them, and did they think Patricia wanted to be part of the group. Mary sounded angry and hurt: "I don't think Patricia wants this group. She's my best friend in floor hockey, but doesn't come here. She lied to me, she told me on Monday that she would be here." Adam paused for some time, eventually sharing his thoughts: "If Patricia was here, I'd ask her what's wrong. One day she'll learn." I interpreted the group's reaction as an expression of their growth. For Mary, finding fault with others who had disappointed her was not something that she had done before. As well, Adam's intuitive feelings about Patricia emerged once again – she did not appear to be aware of how her actions were affecting others.

I was continuing to feel frustrated in my efforts to connect with Patricia even though the next week she showed up. We never seemed to consistently find a way to work with her and while the topic that week (feeling excluded from one's family) was significant to her, she stonewalled us. The discussion began when Jan, the oldest member and one who rarely talked about emotional pain, described her disappointment when her brother did not inform her of the date when her cousin's funeral was to take place: "I could have taken the bus. I wanted to go, but wasn't told. He's protecting me too much." We then asked the others if they felt that having a disability label also meant having one's emotions labeled as that of a perpetual child, as someone who could not cope with grief for example. I turned to Patricia and reminded her that when we first met, we had talked about her feeling different from her sister and asked her whether her parents treated them differently. At first I thought we were going to get somewhere when she acknowledged that was true, but it was quickly followed with an explanation that kept me at bay: "I usually go to my mom and my sister goes to my dad when there's an argument." Nothing out of the ordinary about that dynamic, so I tried another angle: "You both live on your own. Do you think your parents worry more about you or her?" But that did not work either, as Patricia smiled, describing how her mother worries too much about her traveling alone at night – again a normal family occurrence unrelated to having Down's syndrome.

Although Patricia did not appear to be ready to get into this issue, Betty certainly was and with a fiery enthusiasm seemed to suddenly realize that she was also excluded from the family in significant ways: "I have a brother who doesn't call me back. He wouldn't do that with the other sisters. I have a sister as well who doesn't call." Carl too was musing over the way his father bosses him around, telling him what to do all the time and he became energized the more he thought about it, even encouraging Jan to talk to her brother: "You need to tell him he hurt your feelings." I felt the group come alive as they rallied to each other's story with words of defiance and strength, recognizing that they were being cheated of some respect – except Patricia who remained silent until we were almost finished.

We were closing on the topic of feeling excluded at school and without being approached, Patricia jumped in: "Thanks for talking about schools. A long time ago, I was left alone. I was a kid." I asked her how she felt being excluded, to which she replied: "I felt different, the only one in the group." Then Adam asked her if she was disliked because she was different and Patricia acknowledged that to be true. My last question to Patricia was whether being different was lonely. She did not elaborate and there really was no need to. We had heard more vulnerable feelings from her than ever before.

Patricia's attendance continued to be inconsistent as it was for some of the other members of the group. In fact, Mary never returned and the impact of her mysterious disappearance lingered in the group for quite some time. She refused to return our phone calls and had even shunned group members when she saw them at the social events she had referred to so frequently in the group. It was very puzzling for all of us and I felt united with the group in our attempt to understand what might have happened – none of us had seen this coming. Not that we should have been faulted for a lack of prescience, however, I worried that our failure to include

Mary's mother from the beginning of the group's formation was a big mistake. Sara was particularly incensed about Mary's rejection of their association outside of the group and the lame excuse of needing to look after her new cat as a reason for not attending. I wondered in particular what Patricia thought of Mary's disappearance considering the bond that they had, but Patricia was silent on the matter and appeared quite relaxed at the next session.

I tried to pursue Patricia's feelings on the topic of anger, particularly anger towards one's father, and noted how she skillfully foiled my attempts. The topic came up when Sara, who had quite a fiery temper in her past, described the time that she bit her father's hand and then snapped his glasses in half when he meddled in her love life. The group found this story quite amusing, and Patricia muttered under her breath a few times: "That's weird." We then questioned Patricia on the relationship that she had with her father and whether or not she had ever felt angry with him. She responded: "You just wouldn't want to see me when I get angry." She had displayed such little anger in the group that I found it hard to believe her, though it certainly was an intriguing image. I challenged her: "I'm surprised to hear you say that. I've never seen you get angry here." Patricia clarified: "Things go through my mind." I found her comment interesting because we had never really broached the topic of inner thoughts, rather we had focused exclusively on inner *feelings*. As so often happened in our pattern with Patricia, she withheld the details and obfuscated her meaning. "I can't imagine," she replied, when I probed for more details.

It was Carl who was keenly interested in the topic of anger as he delved into descriptions of how his father had beaten his sister, the involvement of the police and the aftermath. Patricia had been listening intently as the story unfolded and complimented Carl on his ability to cope with the situation: "It takes a big person. Take care of yourself, Carl."

Marco and I met with Patricia about one month later as part of an assessment process to determine if group members felt that they were gaining from the group. Patricia's attendance had become quite erratic as had other members', and there were times when I thought the group would dissolve altogether. Her feedback surprised me as she expressed her interest in remaining in the group and the feeling that she had improved as a result of attending. But what was most shocking was when she revealed that she believed Sara and herself were the only people in the group with a developmental disability, because "we both have Down's syndrome". It took a lot of courage to say. This revelation helped explain Patricia's reluctance all these months to talk about that which she identified from the beginning as her goal: standing tall in spite of being disabled. I was chagrined at our oversight, realizing that we had probably never told her that everyone in the group was disabled, assuming that she would know that. Having Down's syndrome was clearly a stigma that she internalized, one that she was ashamed of, that she had learned to bear alone. I wondered how many other individuals would have had the courage to stand tall, as Patricia had learned to do with all of us. It was a proud moment.

Len – Masks
of Denial

"The main reason I'm here is to talk about the problems I'm having with my sister. We fight all the time." Len stayed with this theme for the first three sessions, relentlessly defending that his sole problem in life was beyond his control. Len was one of the youngest members of the group and always wore a baseball cap. He generally had a vacant look as though he was not really paying attention to what was going on. I attributed his disinterest to a lack of experience in discussing emotional issues. Len had told us during his assessment interview that one of his goals was to learn to admit when he was having a problem. I found that significant, especially when he so openly declared the problems with his sister – I thought that somehow we would have to uncover his contribution to it. Len was a soft-spoken man and appeared to keep to himself, reticent about delving into topics that would spark too much debate.

In the first few sessions, Jesse, my co-therapist, and I spoke in generalities about the ease with which we could complain about problematic people in our lives, a convenient means to escape self-reflection. Jesse and I had worked together for years and at the time of the group therapy knew each other well enough that we could say just about anything. We had gone through some harrowing times with disgruntled staff, neighbors trying to abort the group home that Jesse supervised and one very dangerous client who as Jesse described it "embodied all of the seven sins". I was greatly looking forward to working with Jesse because he was so astutely attuned to other's emotions and was thus anxious to uncover those of the new group.

I was hoping that Len would eventually pick up on a theme and reveal something about himself that we could work with, or that some dynamic with another group member would reveal aspects of his personality. But nothing really happened. Well, nothing until my embarrassing blunders with Len surfaced. One of the women had asked him a question and he responded to her with a rather benign reply. I was eager to draw Len into a "here-and-now" process, and jumped at the opportunity to point out how intently he appeared to be staring at me while answering the other participant. I was mortified when Len apologized and then explained that after his eye surgery he could not focus his eyes that well. It was a moment lost – I was too embarrassed to explore my own feelings of stupidity and tactlessness. Nor did I ask Len why he felt he had to apologize and acquiesce when he had done nothing wrong. It was ironic that when I had the opportunity to explore an aspect of Len's personality, I let it slip because of my own weakness. The situation reminded me of how often we as staff blunder through communication with people who are developmentally disabled without having to be accountable to them; the power imbalance in the system often precludes any admission of wrongdoing.

The theme of Len's deferring nature was to emerge again as it became more evident to all of us that he was the "nice guy" in the group. In fact, the group in general was too nice, including Jesse. He carefully thanked the participants for coming and was positively obsequious as they departed, repeatedly thanking each of them for coming. We discussed the fact that as long as our dialogue remained light banter we could never expect the group members to delve into any levels of depth. It was time to stop the ingratiating dialogue.

Slowly, aspects of Len's personality began to emerge and unfold. I was very moved in one session when Len praised Roger's effort to come to the assistance of another participant, Sharon, who was receiving fairly direct and challenging criticism. When Len began his questions with Roger I did not anticipate his motive. In fact, I thought that he was annoyed and angry with Roger for coming to Sharon's rescue. I said to Len: "Why do you want to know what Roger is doing?" He blurted out "Because it's so rare to see someone do something like that. I've hardly ever seen anyone be so nice." It was the last thing I had expected Len to say, having attributed his apparent indifference to a less than compassionate stance. Clearly, I was having difficulty reading Len and had to work to suspend judgment. It reminded me of how often as staff we find ourselves reading through a long file that contains information about the client so that we are armed and ready before even meeting the person. The system rewards such thorough "preparation" and staff quickly learn which clients to avoid based on long lists of "incident reports".

Len continued to develop his presence in the group, his personality becoming less of a mystery. I noted his intensity in feeling, his strive to understand, his sagacious abilities. He emerged in small segments though, agreeing or disagreeing here and there with others' comments and reactions, always keeping his words to a minimum. The first time that we saw Len engaged in a longer discussion was on the topic of anger, a topic that he had willingly tackled with one of the other participants who vehemently denied his anger. Surprisingly, this time Len adopted the same position; he faltered several times and appeared mortified at the idea of being found out, that all might see his subconscious fantasies. The discussion began when I approached both Len and Andrew as to whether or not they felt left out in the group. Len, who characteristically slumped in his chair with his head in his hand, replied: "I'm waiting for someone to ask me that's all. I'm following the rules, the way I was taught." We explored further what *the* rules were and who set them, questioning whether or not they existed in the group. Len seemed to maintain that rules established within his home traveled with him, regardless of the setting. He appeared to believe that a simple explanation of "My parents taught me that way" would suffice our curiosity. Len withdrew even further from the topic when one of the other group members shared his repressed anger towards an abusive stepfather, but Jesse was determined to explore Len's feeling. It was the first time that I had noticed Len getting angry as we probed further about his feelings towards both parents. "It's their house, I follow the rules," Len repeated, hoping this time to avert our questions. Jesse continued: "Is that frustrating?" Suddenly, Len's anger burst forth as he announced that "I beat the crap out of a punching bag in the basement." I tried to help him feel accepted with his confession and remarked ever so gently, almost whispering: "So there's a lot of anger there." But Len seemed to sense what I was after, and appeared to have had enough: "Not a lot," he replied resolutely. What struck me about this exchange was how similar I was to Len, wishing to hide the level of rage that could surface. I was keenly anxious to understand what his anger referenced to.

One of the other group members, perhaps not realizing that Len was closing down, asked if he had ever punched someone in his family. I was afraid that the question was too direct, too bold for Len at this time and anticipated that he would probably reject the subject altogether; I did not want him to expose all of his unconscious urges, just to talk about some of the daily anger common to all in close relationships. Jesse and I were not of the same mind and he eagerly continued with the family theme: "You never thought of giving your sister the one-two?" Len was flustered: "No, well…yes! I've thought of it." I was thrilled to see the allowances he was making and tried a reassuring intervention: "We all have fantasies, if everybody knew them, we'd all be in jail." Ironically, Len's last comment to the group, "I never get angry," was said with quite a bit of anger. I suspected that he felt both frustrated and relieved with the session. I hoped that we had made some progress in drawing him closer, that the pace of the process did not overwhelm him. He somehow seemed so delicate.

While the group struggled with the topic of being labeled "mentally handicapped," Len's reaction was by far the most peculiar and the one that I felt least equipped to respond to. He exhibited a lot of emotion but not about his story – he told someone else's. "I always stood up for the wheelchair kid in high school. Everyone used to tease him and I'd tell the other kids to leave him alone. It was rude. Even the teachers would join in. I just don't understand how adults could do that. But I looked after him, helped him get around and always came to his defense." I was fascinated with the story on many levels. Len was once again demonstrating his genuine compassion and concern for others, a quality that emerged many times in the weeks that I had worked with him. I was surprised that Len had no self-consciousness, as though he had nothing to say about himself because the topic simply did not apply to him. When I probed about his own experience, Len was adamant: "I've never been labeled. I went to a normal high school, I've done everything that normal kids do, I've never been called anything." Was it possible that no one had told him he had a developmental disability or was he in the wrong group? I did not pursue this further in the session, rather I decided that it would be important to give him a chance to talk with us privately. He turned to me just before the group ended in response to my incredulous gaze: "I guess I'll be on the hot seat next week." His comment suggested to me that he was well aware of the deception and wondered if it had worked in keeping us at bay.

Jesse and I both invited Len to help us understand what was going on after the other group members left. Without hesitation he told us the story: "When I was five, a doctor told my parents that there would be a lot of things that I could not do. But I did all those things, so I've just forgotten about being labeled." Jesse and I exchanged knowing glances and thanked Len for sharing that information with us, reassuring him that there would be no pressure to explain anything to the group the following week. But it was a decision that was unfair and confusing to the others. Indeed, one of the group members had asked Len "Weren't you born with a handicap?" to which he replied "Not that I know of, not yet." I was concerned that Len's exclamation of normalcy would disrupt the balance of power and intimacy in the group. Dr.

Shapero advised us to leave the topic for now, that unless Len initiated, we should not in any way attempt to "enlighten" him.

"I've never talked to anyone about this, not even my parents." Len began with a story about an uncle who had died and how heartbroken he was about his loss. I had not expected anything like that to emerge from Len, even though we had been together as a group at that time for nine weeks; still, his openness and confession of deep sorrow was quite out of character relative to his presentation up until then. As sad as the story and surrounding feelings were, it was with some excitement that I listened intently. I was pleased that we might begin to know Len. "My uncle showed me the world. Two years ago, he had a heart attack. I wasn't upset 'til I went to the funeral. Now I think about him a lot. I go to my room and cry. No one else knows about it." Ironically, as Len told the story, his eyes began to sparkle, and he came alive in a way I had never seen before – he seemed relieved to have someone to talk to. I thought to myself, finally we are getting somewhere, unfolding layers of complexity, pain, confusion, and raw emotion that we so often deny persons with a developmental disability. I knew of many clients who were not invited to attend family member's funerals as they were not attributed as feeling grief. I again thought how common it was to never have help in facing the pain of one's disability. I thought that Len had been so shielded from this, perhaps to his detriment, that it could never be addressed. I wondered if the same sigh of relief would be visible on his face if he could also confront his own losses, the loss of a normal life. I drew myself back and asked him if his uncle was like a father to him. He smiled: "Yes, I had two fathers, I wasn't closer to one than the other. My uncle and I put together a 1957 Chevy and I really hope that I'll get that car someday. It would mean so much to me." It struck me how Len transformed as the story continued, how relaxed he became, how comfortable he looked. Len usually sat with a cap on his head, one hand supporting his chin and slumped quite low in his chair. Today, he looked right at me, sat up straight, the hat was absent and his hands were comfortably resting on his chair. He spoke with confidence: "Today I thought I might as well share my feelings. I thought this would be a good place to talk about them."

Len succinctly and insightfully relayed his disappointment with his father for refusing to deal with his own feelings about the loss of his brother-in-law: "It still bothers me that my dad and uncle didn't get along. I don't understand why he can just say to me 'Let it go' when he never wants to talk about my uncle. They didn't get along that well and it really bothers me." Finally, I felt I had some way to enter Len's family, to explore a path that might help him to further develop the relationships that he yearned for, to tread slowly towards his loneliness within the family.

As hoped for, Len did share more about himself the next week – this time it was the loneliness in friendships that he spoke about, and with great eloquence. He was emerging as the most open, insightful and motivated of the group members, quite a turn-around from his initial posture; I wondered how threatening he was becoming to the others as he rose in status in the others' eyes. Gone was the Len who waited for permission to speak and who slouched in his chair with apparent disinterest. He dove in immediately when the session began, challenging one of the women who when asked how she was, always stated, "Fine." "Outside of this room, before the group began you were upset, so how are you fine all of a sudden?" It was not the first time that Len had been intense, but this time he appeared to be increasingly more confident as well. His voice was almost booming as he tactfully queried his peer, showing also a consideration for her distress. He added: "I could see it in her eyes that she was upset and angry."

Len continued to astonish us with his insights and one time, decided to challenge my remarks about how behavior in the group reflects how we behave outside of the group, that the group is a microcosm, a stage in which we play out our drama as we do in the "real" world. Again, he spoke with such confidence: "Sometimes that's wrong though. Here I'm pretty open, but outside I'm not. I only interact with my friends sometimes, and hardly ever with my parents." He was absolutely right, for I had been far too simplistic in my summation and had overlooked his point entirely. I felt so relieved that Len could comfortably challenge my authority, and prove me wrong. Jesse complimented Len on his new way of relating: "I notice that you're not waiting to be asked before you talk. Can you do that outside of the group?" Len threw up his hands slightly, nodding in agreement with Jesse and answered: "That's what I was hoping for. If it works here, I'll try it out there." How well he had stated the goal of therapy and I hoped that all of the members could be so inspired. It was one of the most exciting moments in the course of the project up to that time. I felt proud of Len, proud of the group, and proud of our work.

Len continued to have a powerful impact on the group, especially when he confronted Harold for lying to the group the previous week. His adeptness at managing difficult situations and knowing just what to say soon became apparent. Len doggedly persisted with Harold, insisting that he explain why he lied. Eventually, Len took the risk and expressed his feelings fully as to the effect it had on him: "That pisses me off. I've never lied, well except sometimes to the teachers at school, but not about anything big. [He turned and faced Harold] "It's going to be hard to believe you now." Len was passionate about how Harold had transgressed in a way that I had never seen nor imagined that he was capable of. He really carried the session for Jesse and me, as there was very little to say after such germane observations: "I thought you [Harold] were coming here for friends, open relationships. How can you expect that when you lie? How can you gain our respect when you lie? 'Sorry' doesn't really help. I *did* like you, but now that you've lied." Len looked sad and despondent as he spoke these words. It was clear that his disappointment was not just self-serving, he was also sad for Harold and the group. His words were more powerful than any Jesse and I could utter to Harold; to be indicted by one's peers is infinitely more meaningful than by the designated social worker.

Not only did Len take it upon himself to deal with Harold, he also extended his help to the others by guiding them through the complexity of the process. In particular, he advised one of the women who was reticent to respond and fearful of Harold: "You have to look him in the eye and tell him he's a liar. It happened to me once in school and I had to talk to the guy who lied to me face-to-face. Then it was OK." I was glad that I had deferred to Len to advise her, not just because it was having more impact coming from a peer, but because of his insights – they were better than mine.

Len continued to outpour with emotional strength and openness the following week and wasted no time in doing so. One of the group members had had an epileptic seizure just prior to our starting; she had suffered a bad fall and had to be taken to the hospital due to an injured eye. Len was clearly concerned and shaken by the experience: "Sharon falling reminded me of my dad seizuring and falling out of his chair. My parents didn't tell me until I was 18, when they thought I was man enough, that he had seizures. I used to cry when I saw him seizure, but they never told me what was happening." Jesse remarked on Len's ability to comfortably talk about that which makes him cry, to which Len replied: "I'm never afraid to admit my feelings. If they don't like it, tough for you." I wondered whether or not anyone in Len's family could imagine his transformation or whether we alone were privy to his extraordinary ability to speak his mind.

Ironically, when Peter began to express his negative feelings about his parents, Len had a very difficult time hearing him. Their back and forth revealed many of Len's own fears and apprehensions about exploring his relationship with his parents. It began when I encouraged Peter to tell us more about himself, which he did with relative ease: "I have problems with drinking and went for alcohol treatment. Then I had a relapse but have not had a drink for seven months." I asked: "Did you drink because you were lonely?" Peter replied: "My parents don't care about me at all, so sometimes I drink. They don't call, write, or ever see me. I have to call them. I have bad memories of visiting them at Christmas. It's a bad feeling. I don't want to go there." Len's voice was booming and he startled us with his diatribe: "Every parent cares. They care but they don't want to spend time with you. Have you asked if they care?" Peter was feeling the pressure, but trying to explain: "Yes, they say they're too busy. I say it's an excuse. I'm going to phone them tonight." Len appeared somewhat satisfied: "Yeah, talk to them." I felt it was important for the group to accept Peter's feelings, that we should avoid all effort to problem-solve, to reduce the emotion to a scripted, linear trajectory; I was addressing Len in particular as he was clearly uncomfortable with the image of a broken family. I turned to him and said: "Len, why do you defend all parents?" He looked at me as though I had missed an important point: "My parents love me, all parents love their children." I found myself debating with him: "The world isn't that perfect." Len exclaimed: "It is, even bank robbers who are parents love their children. My parents gave me the world, all parents give something." Len was practically leaping out of his chair, anxious to prove his point and for the others to agree with him. Peter remained silent.

I thought it was ironic that Len was defending family when his original goal for group therapy was to deal with his sister, but I was getting nowhere in my attempt to convince him of Peter's perspective. Peter had remained quiet throughout my dialogue with Len and when we both paused, exhausted for words, he shared what must have been his most painful secret: "After I was born, my parents sent me to an institution because I was blind. After Orillia, I lived in a nursing home in Barrie. My parents treated me terribly when I was a child." Len was shocked, and no sooner had Peter finished his sentence, then he apologized: "It kind of makes me feel bad. It seems like not all parents are the same. I really feel stupid now." I turned to Len: "I like your honesty about admitting to feeling stupid." In fact, his honesty and ability to retract from a position that he had so vehemently defended, and all within about 15 minutes, shocked me. Len answered modestly: "Well, it finally clicked." Jesse and I relished in the moment of genuine contact and did not feel the need to respond.

Len had missed the session before our Christmas break, so when we commenced the group in January, it had been a month since I had last seen him. I was nervous that he might be wavering in his commitment like Harold was. I felt relieved when I saw him sitting in the circle waiting for Jesse and me to arrive, yet with his cap returned to its position on his head. Something seemed off – either he was depressed or unenthusiastic about being back and when asked how he was, Len responded with a flat affect: "Nothing new, same old me." I replied: "It sounds like you wish there was something different." Len jumped up as though he had suddenly been injected with a burst of energy and with a loud voice said: "Yeah, I wish I had a new life! I wish I had a girlfriend. I wish my dad wasn't so strict. I wish he'd change. I want to move away but I can't 'cause I don't get paid enough. My dad has changed. He wants this done and that done and I have no control over it." I was taken aback, not so much by the long list of complaints, but by his openness and willingness to bare his soul so quickly. I felt good about the level of trust that prompted him to speak as he had.

As we had also not seen the others in quite some time, we moved on until everyone had a chance to give us an update. We had important unfinished business to attend to with one of the participants whose mother had called me, and spent considerable time trying to sort that out. Len was patiently waiting and coped with his frustration by shutting down, appearing somewhat disinterested in the dialogue, until Amy relayed how hard it was for her to speak when full of emotion: "When you have tears, and it chokes in your throat, you have to wait until the emotions go out." Len claimed emphatically: "I don't do that. If someone pisses me off, I tell them, unless it's a fist fight."

Dr. Shapero pointed out in our supervision that we had missed an opportunity to link Len's comment to his opener – he had not been able to confront his father. Rather, Jesse and I were caught up in the exchange between Sharon and Len, mainly because I had never seen Sharon so alive, so active and so engaging. She was enjoying challenging Len as their exchange went back and forth:

Sharon:	"I don't like arguing."
Len:	"Why not?"
Sharon:	"You don't get anywhere."
Len:	"Yes you do. Lots of times."
Sharon:	"Maybe you think so. I don't."
Len:	"I've argued and then resolved it."
Sharon:	"It's not nice to argue."

Jesse suggested that they were arguing right then and there, at which Sharon protested, and Len immediately agreed. Eventually, they both tired of the discourse realizing that it was indeed an argument and neither of them was prepared to lose. Len seemed to be enjoying it far less than Sharon and because it was new growth for her, the focus of my attention was directed to her, and not Len. We never returned to the theme of Len's father in this session which I felt was a careless mistake on our part. It reflected in Len's weary sigh and response towards the end of the session when Sharon made another attempt to engage him in an argument: "I have nothing to say."

Determined that Len would have an opportunity to talk about the conflict with his father, I kept him in mind from the beginning of the session, waiting for an opportune time. When someone started talking about getting a job outside of the city, Len surprised me by saying: "I wouldn't want to move out there 'cause I'll never leave my mom and dad." I turned to him with an incredulous look and said: "That's different from last week. You wanted to move." He replied: "Yeah, but not very far away. I feel secure with them. I need them to be there if I need help." Immediately, I thought back to the time when Len had denied that he had a disability and while any 21-year-old may have said the same thing, I knew that "help" meant a lot more than emotional or financial support. I presumed that Len was dependent on his parents for all kinds of things related to his disability yet continued to skirt around this issue.

As Len launched into a description of how difficult his father was, I suspected that it would be dangerous to jump in the middle and take a side – clearly Len and his father needed to be present for any meaningful assessment to take place. However, I thought that the process of talking about his emotions, both for the benefit of himself and the other members of the group, was vital. His intensity certainly came through: "More and more, my dad is getting harder. He might kick me out. Once you're a certain age, he has it in his mind that you have to leave home. But, I'm not ready." As the others listened intently, Len continued: "I'm kind of scared. In two or three years I'll be ready, but not now. I know my mom loves me. She said I can stay. I'm afraid my dad will say 'bye' in two months." I felt that the best way to help Len might be to explore whether he had shared his feelings with his father: "Have you told him that?" Len seemed almost startled at the idea: "No! I'm afraid there'll be a big argument. My sister once argued for three weeks with him. My mom says I should tell him, but I won't. I love him. I don't want to argue." Len looked around at all of our faces and I imagined felt vulnerable about putting his feelings so close to our scrutiny: "I didn't want to bring this up, but I guess I had to." I reassured him, and so did the other participants by talking about their living situations and how they had dealt with their own leaving of their parents' home. The group had grown quite close, there was an ease in the way they talked to, supported and nurtured each other.

I felt one of the more helpful moments for Len was when I shared my own fears with him: "One thing that we can help you with is exploring some of your feelings about what it might be like to live on your own. I know how scary it can be. I was really scared when I left home." Len looked at me and jumped back with some relief: "Oh. OK!" Then Andrew who rarely spoke about his emotions, without being prodded, joined in: "I'm scared too. If my mom retires soon and there's no job for her, or if she passes away soon, then I'll have to move out too." I was struck at how often persons with developmental disabilities are required to move and frequently get used to new living situations, particularly having to leave the family home.

We added two new members to the group the following week and I was counting on Len to be helpful in welcoming them to the group, but he was sullen and reserved. When queried about how he was doing Len burst forward with a loud voice: "I'm mad. This guy I don't even know wanted to get in a fight. I wanted to stand up for Andrew." Andrew was also seething with rage: "He called me 'chink' and threatened my parents." Len continued: "I tried to tell him off 'cause I don't like to see my friends in trouble." I had never seen Andrew so intense, either positively or negatively: "I'm ready to kill him and Len is my witness. I want to kill him. I swear to God I will." I asked both of the men why they had not volunteered their feelings when we started the group; it was obvious from the moment we began that an inordinate amount of tension was choking the room. They explained their taciturn beginnings: "I tried to forget it" and "I was thinking that the more I speak the angrier I'll get." I launched into an explanation about how important it was for everyone to tell us if they're feeling a strong emotion in the group because it would not go unnoticed. My pedantic attempt seemed to have little impact and I thought I was sounding like a schoolteacher. Len brought up his punching bag and how useful it was to him when he needed to unload, although he also agreed that it was useful to confront the person verbally – everyone that is, but his father: "There's only one person I don't get angry with and that's my dad. He'll just say if you're angry, then leave." The discussion continued as other group members tentatively probed Len about his anger and when it came to his mother, he denied ever having been angry with her at all. I thought that admission to be rather sad, and in spite of Jesse's gentle suggestion that no one could live life without ever being mad at their mother, Len remained adamant: "Why should I be angry with her. I love her. She gives me the world." Towards the end of the session, I raised an issue with Len that had me somewhat worried. I had received a call earlier in the week from a staff member, Suzanne, who said that she was working with Len and that his parents had wanted information as to the nature of the group. Her tone was slightly negative and I was imagining the worst – Len, now bolstered with a new confidence and an assertiveness, was going home and running into problems with his parents who might be looking for someone to blame. I nervously rolled the possible scenarios in my mind. When I told Len that his worker wanted to talk, I offered him the opportunity to join us, to which he readily agreed: "I don't want my parents to know what I say here. It's my anger and I want to deal with it here. When I told them that I come here to talk about my problems they said 'Why? You don't have any problems.' They wonder why I can talk to the group here and not to them." Len continued on, complaining about the worker and how she refused to call him back when he told her that he was not happy with the way she was excluding him from decisions with his parents: "She never called me back. I told her not to screw up my life. I'm still angry about it. I feel like she's given up on me." I took a different turn with the subject and asked Len if he would be comfortable telling me if I said or did something that bothered him. "No, I respect my elders, but with Suzanne it went on and on, so I said forget it and told her outright. I don't care if she's the Queen of England, but with you, I don't know you that well." I tried to reassure Len that confronting me was a good thing and that it would be safe to do that in the group, but again, I felt my message was just talk and no one was really convinced that it would be safe. Perhaps I was seen as just another fixture in the system, even after all these months.

I was shocked and dismayed when I spoke to Suzanne, and she relayed that Len had been having psychiatric problems related to thoughts of delusion and suicidal talk. I had viewed Len as one of the more stable individuals in the group and never suspected that he was struggling to such a degree. I quickly agreed that we all should meet the parents, Len, Suzanne, myself and Dr. Shapero. I thought I would never view him in the same way, but when we launched into the topic of crying at the next session, I put aside the notion that Len had deceived us, knowingly or unknowingly.

Maureen had been in a lot of pain for months as she continued to fight with staff over how to care for herself and her dying partner. When she relayed to us that her anger had gotten the better of her and she had thrown a knife at one of the staff, we all gave her harsh feedback. Len's tone was at the same time disapproving and sympathetic: "It wasn't right what you did. I feel sorry about your problems, but then talk about it." The discussion continued for quite some time as each member was given the opportunity to speak to Maureen. There was clear discomfort at having to confront such a seemingly gentle member of the group – quite different from the time when Harold had been dealt with for lying. When we approached Maureen later to see how she was feeling, her tears began to flow as the feelings of frustration and sadness welled up. The discomfort within the group was palpable as now Maureen's tears soon turned to sobbing. I asked the other women if they were able to cry when upset. Amy said: "I like to keep it in. When I see people cry, it makes me cry." Sharon then disclosed the most personal detail that I recalled hearing from her: "Sometimes I wake up laughing or crying." Len was quite interested: "Because of your dreams?" "Probably," she replied. I told Sharon that I believed she was more free with her emotions when asleep rather than awake. I remember feeling shocked that Sharon, who was often so lifeless and devoid of intensity, would experience a range of intense emotions in her dreams.

When I asked Len if he was free enough to cry, he did not hesitate to answer: "I cry a lot. I think of my dead uncle and it makes me very upset. I go to bed crying almost every night. My parents wonder why, but I don't tell them. My father might get angry that he's just an uncle and say to me 'I'm your father'." My thoughts went back to Suzanne's comments and I wondered if it was all a misinterpretation – maybe no one in the family understood Len or knew that his pain made "sense".

It was clear as the discussion continued that most members of the group felt they could not cry with anyone in view, a problem that seems endemic to our society, and not necessarily unique to the person with a developmentally disability. But, I believe that the acknowledgement of complex emotions, such as grief, deep sadness, mourning the loss of a normal life, is not part of the professional's repertoire, and may not be part of the family's repertoire. The desire to smooth over the feelings of loss for the disabled person is our attempt to feel better and to find an optimistic angle to what is, at times, a very painful and frustrating life.

Amy relayed a very interesting story about how she coped with crying and I thought it indicative of how well-intentioned professionals had inadvertently denied her expression. She began by saying: "I hide in the washroom if I cry. I don't like other people to see me cry." Sharon asked why. "I don't know. The only person who might know is my mother, if I disappear in my room and then come out. She can tell by my eyes. If I'm at a funeral, I make sure that I'm in the front so no one's looking at me." It was unusual for Amy to divulge such detail about how she organized her thoughts and what sort of emotions emerged. We were all captivated by her prodigious disclosure. She continued: "When I was volunteering at camp, the minister said when you're upset, pray to God behind closed doors. Let your tears be between you and God. So I make sure now that no one sees it." Peter was the first to express amazement: "'Cause when you're talking to God you cry behind closed doors?" The stories of crying all alone evoked a plaintive image that stayed with me for the rest of the group and I felt it was important to share with them my own discomfort: "It took me a long time to feel comfortable crying in front of others and for me to learn that it was helpful to be with people." There was a knowing silence that we all shared.

The first time that I led the group alone occurred when Jesse took a holiday in Peru. I was acutely aware of my nervous stomach and expected that the group would slow down, maybe even regress – I anticipated a disaster. The beginning was somewhat reminiscent of the first session when Len opened with: "I'm losing control with my sister. I'm actually sticking up for myself, but I don't want to 'cause I don't want to be rude to her." He elaborated further: "I've even sworn at her a couple of times – it's a new thing. I don't know why it's happening. I used to keep my mouth shut." I was wary of accepting Len's story based on the caution I had received from his worker, but gave him the benefit of the doubt on the next piece: "We almost got into a fist fight and I never want that to happen. I told her sorry, but you're pushing me off the cliff! I'm old enough to stick up for myself." I decided to broaden the agenda to a theme of standing up for oneself and asked the others what they were struggling with in that area. Amy reticently described how it was hard for "girls" to stand up to "guys" and when I probed to find out if she was talking about herself, she eventually admitted that it was her boyfriend. The further we got into the discussion, the more we were all alarmed at what we were hearing. Slowly, the details began to emerge about the physical and verbal abuse that she was receiving from her boyfriend: "He wants his own way," "He puts me down sometimes," "He hits me and calls them love taps."

Catherine, one of the new members, had been badly beaten by a boyfriend six months previously and was currently facing the possibility of a court appearance, so her reaction to Amy's story was intense: "Get completely rid of him before you get hurt and have a black eye and scars. It happened to me. Drop him." While Len offered Amy caring advice such as, "If it hurts, you should leave him, totally get rid of him," he wove his own guilt and sorrow with his sister into the dialogue. I noted that I had never seen him so bothered before about his own actions. Perhaps, all the talk of violence, especially men towards women, was pricking his conscience: "Well, it finally comes out. I hit my sister, but I did say I was sorry. I actually started to cry. Me hitting someone? I'm not that kind of person." Little did we know that Len *was* that kind of person.

The meeting with Len and his parents was very revealing and quite shocking. The Len at home was very different from the Len in-group and it took quite a lot of mental adjusting to fit both of them in the same body. We began the meeting by letting his parents know our concerns about Len's sister based on what he had told us – her abusive, taunting and unrelenting teasing, all of which was driving him to tears on a regular basis. Len's father stared straight at us, rather than looking at his son and replied emphatically: "That isn't true at all. He never knows when to quit trying to get our attention. He just won't leave her alone. He pulls at her hair and pushes her in the rocking chair and walks away laughing." There were many more contradictions exposed from the stories Len had told us over the past four months and the realities that his parents portrayed. Len's mother commented on how reclusive he was, his inability to make friends, and how terrible his school experience had been based on the merciless teasing that he received over many years. Even more startling was the description of Len pacing in his room until 4:00 and 6:00 a.m., talking to himself, including a dialogue about suicide. Len admitted that it was true, that he felt there was nothing to live for at one time, but that he would never think that way again.

Len was also described as having rages where he subjected the family to a series of profanities in the form of abusive threats and how he damaged property in the house. Len claimed to not remember any of this. I found his protestations of "amnesia" believable, as he was so honest about all the rest. There was very little defensiveness on his part once everything was said and we looked to him for verification. "Well, now you know everything about me," he commented towards the end of the meeting. We reassured Len and his parents that he was doing extremely well in the group and that we would continue to help him. I felt very compassionate towards him when he admitted to having a great fear of success, having been used to so much failure. I realized we had overlooked the possibility that Len's leadership position and positive interaction with others in the group was in actuality very difficult to bear. As he put it: "I'm used to being on the bottom."

Not only was being on "top" a position that he had never carried before, it was also evoking fears of loss: "I'm afraid that I'll be alone again after the group has finished." Len's mother confirmed that he had no friends, was quite reclusive other than family members, and was unable to approach anyone for company. It was agreed that another meeting, this time with Len and his sister, would be critical; she was leaving home for the first time to live in her own apartment and Len was having tremendous separation anxiety and feelings of rejection.

I was quite anxious about how the next session would go, wondering how much Len was going to admit to the group and how far to push him if he decided to hide out. I launched into a pedantic tactic by listing the benefits of revealing one's soul as a subtle means of spurring Len on: "Amy, we got to know you just a little bit more last week and slowly we built our connection with you. It's hard to really know people. We all want to be seen in a certain way. This group is different from a social group that way. Here the main thing is to show your face of sadness or fear, or whatever it may be." Len looked bored and vacant and the others only muttered rote responses – no one was biting. Eventually, Amy brought up her abusive boyfriend again and both Catherine and Len repeated their sentiments from the previous session where this first emerged. When I asked Len what he was thinking about, he confidently replied: "Things are getting better." Sharon was puzzled: "Are you still fighting with your sister?" I thought this might be his moment of truth, but on the contrary, Len sounded strange: "Nope. I don't know how to explain it. Now I'm actually smiling. I woke up and felt a hundred percent. I usually feel that no one wants me or cares, but I've felt good all week. My parents can't believe it." He continued to carry on with the wellness bravado as we all stared with reservation: "Some weeks I don't want to get out of bed, my life is so boring. But lately, I feel like a bundle of joy. I feel like I own the world. I decided to bring it up 'cause I feel so great about myself." He also divulged that his sister was opposed to the idea of the three of us meeting, which developed into a fascinating discussion about how it feels to be

talked about in meetings with staff or parents. I felt uncertain on
how to challenge Len and whether it was even appropriate, so I
decided to let the group pursue the topic of resenting caregivers.
Len reveled in the topic, as did Catherine: "Counselors are so
nosey. I tell them that but it goes in one ear and out the other. I
hate them. I feel so angry." The energy continued to build to an
intensity that I had never seen before – everyone was jumping in
with something and Len had no trouble embellishing: "I can't get
my parents out of my life. I wish they'd disappear. They're always
bugging me. They'll always ask me 'Were you nice or mean
today?' They're always keeping an eye on me. One day, I'll trick
them and be a bad boy. They'll freak and I'll laugh at them." I
watched Len nervously, still failing to stop him. There was a slight
uneasiness that was palpable as the women attempted to lighten
his threats. When the session ended, I felt confused about what to
do. It was clear that Len strongly needed to maintain his image of
"king", as he once referred to himself in the group.

Len continued on with his bravado at the next session and this
time it had to do with his social life: "I'd love to live on my own.
I'd get a maid to clean my apartment and whip me up a good
dish." Sharon smiled: "Maybe a wife would do it." Len replied:
"I'll never get married. I had seven girlfriends and now my present
girlfriend is too bossy." This was not anything close to the Len
that his parents had presented at our meeting. However, I adopted
the same tactic as the previous week and decided that if I challenged him, it would be too humiliating. I was also impressed
with the process in the group, how astute Sharon was with her
questioning, and her persistence with Len to find out more about
what was going on.

Sharon: "You don't like bossy women? Why?"

Len: "The man should be in charge. Well, not always.
            The woman could be in charge as well. This is
            my seventh break up. After this, I'll give up for
            good. My parents being bosses is enough. My

girlfriend doesn't understand what I'm mad about."

I interjected: "What are you mad about?"

Len: "Everyone controls me. I'm a grown man. I don't have any space at all."

I felt that I had no control with Len anymore either. He seemed free in a way to our responses, maybe too free. "I feel like dying. I want to be with my uncle. When that day comes, I'll be so happy. I'd love to have a car run over me so I could be with him. I loved him like a father." Len said all of this with a smile and I wondered if his talk of suicide was a ploy to avoid dealing with who he really was. He made sure that we were left with yet another negative impression of his sister before the session ended when I asked him what he was hoping for at our upcoming meeting with her. "The last time we had a meeting, she yelled at me, it's gonna be scary. If she gets mad, she might use words you don't like – foul language."

Later that evening I met with Len and his infamous sister, Tara, curious about the "monster" that had been described to all of us over the course of the past six months. Tara was as curious about what was going on as I was and when asked what I could do for them, she seemed surprised, as though she was the one who had been summoned. "I'm here for Len," was all she said before he jumped in with full force. I sat back and watched for the next 30 minutes as Len berated Tara about how she had neglected him by moving out of the parental home and dropping a boyfriend whom Len had gotten along with. To all of his criticisms, she responded with a concern, patience, and consideration, beyond what most of us could reasonably tolerate given the circumstance. It was Len at his worst. I felt guilty for having judged Tara harshly at times and, even worse, felt duped by Len. Her dedication appeared genuine and solid. She was quite hurt at having been portrayed as a whip-cracking tyrant and asked Len why he would have ever conveyed such an image. He appeared slightly embarrassed and threw out several examples of how often she had forced him to do the dishes or help with other household chores.

Like so many siblings of developmentally disabled brothers and sisters, Tara had assumed some of the parental role and had also absorbed a lot of guilt because of her relative good fortune, to have been given a normal life. I was relieved when the meeting was over, not so much because of my own apprehensions, but because I felt that I finally understood Len. The pieces of the puzzle were making more sense and I felt that I would be far more effective in helping him. I was particularly pleased when Tara commented that she had never seen Len so articulate and open about his feelings since joining the group and how pleased she was with his progress. Despite the fact that she was the punching bag for those freed up emotions, she had nobly accepted her position. Perhaps, she also needed to learn to express her emotions to Len.

For the next two sessions Len talked about the death of his grandmother who had died a sudden and gory death as a result of an accident. During those sessions, he reminded me of the Len I had seen at the beginning – intensely expressive about his relationship to *someone else*. "My dad wants to be alone now. I was thinking I should ask Jenny [one of Len's group leaders] about what to say to him. I feel stuck in the middle. Every night I go to bed crying. I wish I was in heaven with my grandmother." It seemed that as long as he could include family members in the discussion, he was able to express himself more freely. If the group focus diverted to Len, without any apparent reason other than to gain insight, he still felt too threatened. During the remaining sessions, Len continued to talk about how to interact with his parents throughout the session and the group responded with great warmth, sympathy, and concern for him. It was satisfying to be able to sit back, take a less central role and observe how skillfully Sharon, Andrew, and Peter assumed the responsibility of Len's grieving. When I asked Len if he felt supported and safe in the group he replied, "Yeah, as soon as I came into the room."

Harold – Trial by Fire

When Jesse and I first interviewed Harold's worker, we were given the impression that Harold was going to be difficult, impetuous, and unruly. Her description was laced with numerous examples of his sexual escapades and failure to get through the workshop program in previous years. He had apparently attended a type of employment training center for several years and had dropped out before he was deemed "employable". I was curious to meet Harold especially after hearing about his encounters with so many women. The worker went into great detail about Harold's romantic intentions and we were under the impression that she was unduly captivated. I had attended a number of workshops on sexuality training as it pertained to working with the developmentally disabled and felt somewhat prepared to handle a client whose sexual needs were more at the surface. The training was unusual in the sense that it was not a boring information session; rather it involved experiential participation including lots of role plays. Questions concerning "when to intervene," "sex education vs. sexuality," "what is acceptable sexual behavior" were continuously raised and pondered on. We often struggled to get comfortable with the topic and to articulate some of the more profound issues that haunted all of us when it came to our clients' sexuality. For many of the staff, there was an unconscious attempt to ignore and deny that the sexuality of the clients was present, in spite of our vehement outrage at many of the parents who refused to let their son or daughter grow up. While many of the staff believed themselves to be liberal in their thinking, they were often doing everything they could to avoid dealing with sexual issues. Public masturbation, birth control, privacy, and parental outrage were tall orders to tackle and, usually, quite politically risky.

Most of my concern was focused on whether or not Harold was suitable for our group, as the two individuals from the workshop that we had just interviewed were not and we were concerned about finding eight suitable participants. By the time we decided to approach the workshop staff to see if any of their "trainees" would be eligible for group therapy our overall number was too low to justify three groups. It was extremely important that we start with three groups so that all four of us could participate as group leaders. I also wanted to provide this unique opportunity to at least 20 individuals and we did not want our groups larger than eight.

When a very handsome, mild-mannered individual entered the room, I was expecting a Don Juan character to unfold. Harold was quite mistrustful of Jesse and I, as well as being naturally guarded about his shortcomings. He described his interest in the group in such a way that it appeared as though he was coming to escape from the boredom of the workshop. Harold also wanted us to perceive him as "normal", superior to his fellow workshop peers in intellect and social ability. I found myself silently agreeing with his self-assessment and wondered if the staff at the training centre had made an embarrassing faux pas by enlisting this man who was not developmentally delayed. Still, I was cautious having experienced Len's denial – I too was on guard. After several comments by Harold about his "degree" from a community college, I felt it was important to question him about his disability. I felt badly when Harold immediately dropped his head in embarrassment and said "What would take you a day to learn would take me a week." He went on to describe other problems such as his struggle with alcohol and the rehabilitation through Alcoholics Anonymous, fights with his father and girlfriend and bouts of depression which necessitated the need for ongoing individual psychotherapy. It felt awkward to me that Harold had been forced to declare his disability and, at the same time, I saw that by doing so Harold was able to tell us who he really was and what pained him.

Harold was extremely articulate and descriptive about his life and displayed insight about his personality and character that was remarkably frank and thoughtful. I felt strongly that we could help him though, but I also felt somewhat intimidated by his maturity; I hoped that Jesse and I were up to the task. I wondered whether or not he would find the groups too basic, if the other group members would be viewed as inferior. Harold was clearly experienced with therapy and appeared to be well acquainted with the ways and means of therapists. In the end, Jesse and I came to the conclusion that it was unlikely Harold would ever attend a group. We felt certain that he was not motivated to participate for the right reasons – we doubted that his interest was genuine and that the group was merely a convenient distraction.

Thus, when Harold did not show up for the first session, we were somewhat disappointed but not surprised and attributed his absence to a general problem with commitment. It was striking how quickly we had him "assessed". And even though his worker left a message that he called in sick, I was still skeptical and certain that Harold was gone. My frustration was compounded by the fact that another group member had failed to show at the first session as well. Both Jesse and I felt insecure about the poor attendance and profusely thanked those who did show up fearing the whole project could collapse. So when both Harold and Richard arrived on time for session two we were pleasantly surprised and carefully worked our way through the group to include them in the process.

Harold jumped in with lots of advice for the other participants as though he had known them all for a long time. His need to appear competent was certainly evident as we had seen in his interview. I reserved judgment on whether or not his advice-giving was also related to an innate compassion combined with a feeling of superiority. Regardless, the others received him fairly well, although they appeared to be overwhelmed by his abilities at times and may have been relieved when he suffered a "fall" towards the end of the session. When one of the male group members described his frustrations with an old girlfriend, the discussion veered to the topic of comparing the behavior of men versus women in intimate relationships. Harold was quick to commiserate with him, stating that women could not be trusted. He triggered both myself and, in particular, one of the other women in the group who shot back that men were also untrustworthy. I found myself silently reviewing the stories of his sexual behavior and thinking that his comments were in keeping with his exploitation of women.

Harold returned the next week sullen, withdrawn and somewhat depressed. I attributed his mood to a depression resulting from circumstances outside of the group. However, the mood of the entire group seemed to be both reflective and withdrawn which led me to pursue a line of questioning concerning the present dynamics. After some probing comments, Harold confessed that he had left last week's session very worried that I had thought he was a "jerk" because of his comments about women and that probably the other women in the group were also angry. Once he described his fear and received reassuring, honest feedback, Harold's withdrawn demeanor dramatically changed as he sighed with some relief. It was an important exchange in our relationship because I identified with his vulnerability and respected his courage to ask where he stood. He was also self-critical in a positive sense – he knew his comments were tactless and somewhat offensive and wanted to be told so.

Harold surprised me when he decided to give critical feedback to one of the women in the group who was particularly withdrawn and silent, often refusing to answer direct questions. His sensitivity and assertiveness combined was impressive and he thrived on the positive feedback he received from me for his efforts. Additionally, he confessed at the end of the session that he often wished to take on the identity of Luke Perry, a teenage actor who portrayed the ultimate in West Coast cool, which led to a very important discussion in the group the following week

I was not sure what had happened between Harold and the rest of the group during session five for quite some time. We began the hour by talking about one of the members who had attended the first session and then never came back. There was some debate as to why, and when Harold offered his opinion, I challenged him as he had been absent at that session and had never met the individual. I suspected that Harold's feelings had been hurt by my comments and considering the position he held in the group, he may have been angry with me for pointing out his effort to look competent. When I apologized for embarrassing him, he was quick to deny that he had any emotional response, especially anger. For some reason, Harold decided to take a firm stance that he never felt angry. That triggered a discussion that would last the remainder of the hour as we all felt it necessary to challenge Harold. Upon reflection, I felt that this session was very important for him and not because he finally admitted to having angry feelings. Rather, it seemed to be significant to the group process that Harold was challenged, albeit with hesitation and tentativeness. One by one, the group members told him that "everyone feels anger sometimes". Two sessions earlier one of the women in the group had commented that Harold was always right in line behind Jesse and me – clearly the group recognized his leader role.

Why Harold would not budge from his position on never being angry up until the last ten minutes of the session was puzzling. I left feeling manipulated and out-smarted and also quite confused about who Harold was. Dr. Shapero hypothesized that Harold may have a character disorder because he seemed to enjoy being polemic and his final acquiescence was probably done to appease us. Harold certainly appeared to be disingenuous for the entire hour. The other interesting question that Dr. Shapero posed was: "Is Harold really handicapped?" I decided to phone his worker and tactfully pose the question as to whether or not he had a recent assessment on file, as I was also beginning to have my doubts.

When the two psychological reports arrived I quickly and anxiously read through them. I especially felt the weight of responsibility to help him when I came to the end and read "His prognosis is poor." It was not apparent as to why this was so and in part I regretted reading the assessment because it was somewhat discouraging, although I certainly reserved some hope for Harold. Professional pride is a danger that I have tried to be sensitive to; we often like to see the client improve because of the positive reflection on ourselves, even at times, to the detriment of the client. Once, a behavior therapist that I was working with had so much attachment to the success of her program that she refused to see the client when it was discontinued. The client was so hurt that she regressed and deeply resented the staff, blaming them for destroying her relationship with this therapist. I had also recently read Irvin Yalom's book *Love's Executioner* (1989) in which he described a case where his own hubris became the overriding motive to "help" the patient and how it backfired. I was certainly invested in Harold's success, particularly when the workshop counselor telephoned me to determine if Harold was truant or indeed coming to the group. She expressed some surprise when I reaffirmed that he was faithfully attending every session and felt proud that we had already beaten the odds. Perhaps the most important impression that I was left with upon finishing both reports, was that Harold had, up to this point, hidden his deeper insecurities, such as his concerns about his image and a terrible fear of being perceived as inadequate. He was acutely self-conscious about being labeled, as many others had confessed.

When Len and Andrew began to describe their conflict with family members, and for Len an abusive relationship with a stepfather, Harold was anxious to jump in. The session had begun when one of the women gave Harold some direct feedback about his lack of eye contact (interestingly, this was also mentioned in the psychiatric assessment) and the way he held his hand up around his mouth when speaking. Her pluck was a surprise to me and the other group members although in the last session Harold's resolute stance on anger had been slowly dismantled under group pressure. Harold first replied with "That's how I talk," but after I gently asked him how it felt to be in a different position in the group, to not be the leader but the recipient, he immediately understood and without further explanation added "It's a change, normally I don't get feedback." He continued: "I get nervous when I look at people's faces. I can't look at them when I talk to them."

The session continued on another important topic, the relationship between the men in the group and their fathers. It began when one of the more quiet members talked about why he was so shy and relayed that it was because of an abusive relationship with a stepfather. Interestingly, he was not able to say the relationship was abusive until Harold asked him directly. I thought that Harold had raised this question because of his extensive experience in therapy and it seemed to be the question that everyone gets asked and maybe the one that he had repeatedly been asked about. It was not until I received the psychiatric reports that I learned he also had an abusive relationship with his father. After sympathetic and supportive comments to Andrew were expressed by several group members, Harold summed it up with such pathos: "It would be nice if he could take you in his arms and tell you that he loves you."

After Harold's earlier admission about his difficulty with eye contact, I was certainly more cognizant of it and studied him carefully for the first few minutes at the start of our session. Harold always played with the wires leading to his headphones, his gaze averted in the direction of his lap with one leg crossed on top of the other. He was impeccably groomed, every strand of hair in exactly the right place with a precise amount of gel in it, and his clothing particularly neat. I wanted to watch him for any other nonverbal patterns that I had missed. When Jesse recapitulated the previous session, reminding Harold of the important feedback that he had received, Harold added that he also had a tendency to talk too fast and too much. I noted that Harold could often describe his behaviors with accuracy but would with great reluctance include his feelings as though to satisfy us. So when Jesse prodded persistently, Harold was able to disclose that getting the feedback from a "girl" was particularly embarrassing and that it would have been easier to hear from a "guy". He had such a tremendous fear of looking fatuous, especially to a woman. I was impressed with his openness, his eventual willingness to relinquish his defenses, to bear the deeper feelings. Jesse and I were optimistic that in spite of the odds against Harold participating, we had succeeded and were off to a good start.

When the topic turned to the feelings associated with being labeled, I felt it was the first time that we had resonated with Harold's deepest loss. Of all the participants in the group, he was the only one to acknowledge that he had a label relating to his cognitive difficulties; everyone else skirted around it and chose to talk about other labels that they had been saddled with. Peter put his blindness first; Maureen talked about how physically slow she was; Kathy described the pain of being an epileptic; Mark, the racial slurs he had heard because he was Filipino, and Len denied ever having been labeled with anything. It was intensely painful, yet fascinating to see each person protect the most humiliating label of all – the development disability. Considering the time when Harold had so vehemently denied his anger and held out against the admonishment of all the others, his prowess in admitting to being a "slow learner" was surprising – it was the closest anyone came to the mental retardation label. I thought back to my first interview with him and how ashamed he must have been to have to admit his handicap. The story he told was a poignant description of what must have occurred many times throughout his life. "My mom and dad were talking to my uncle about his life as a pilot. I told him that I wanted to be like him – a pilot. He turned to me and said but you're comparing apples to oranges. You could never be a pilot because of your disorder." I expected Harold to then tell us how tremendously painful it was to hear those words and to have so many dreams shattered, but he brushed off our concern with "Nothing's impossible." Still, we praised him for sharing such an intimate story, which he seemed to appreciate, and questioned whether or not he had been worried that people might laugh at him. I knew that it would be important for Jesse and I to go back to this topic and to tackle or surface the feelings that must have been masked behind the label. One could only imagine the hundreds of times that Harold and the others had suppressed their feelings, even with the staff of an agency whose focus was the disabled.

At the next group Harold attended, he fired at everyone with caustic, sardonic words that stunned us all. I reeled from the emotional intensity and trauma for many hours afterwards and was very worried that Jesse and I had not done enough during the session to manage the potential damage he had instilled. I felt a little reassured when the observers gave us feedback that we had done all that we could, but afterwards, the fear of having failed the other participants and the disillusionment I felt about Harold was prominent. I began to write about it late at the office that same day, hoping that I could regain my balance and better understand what had happened and what my role in the drama was.

Prior to the group starting, Jesse and I had discussed the importance of reviewing with the group their feelings about the previous week's topic of having a label as a disabled person. We knew that it was unfinished on many levels and would probably be revisited throughout the life of the group. Amy had left describing the pain of being called a "big fat pig" in the final ten minutes of the session; Jesse and I both felt that it was important to give her and the others a chance to review those feelings, as time had not permitted our full response.

When Amy swept in the room looking particularly well dressed and proudly asked: "How do I look?" with a confident smile, I was relieved to see that she was in an optimistic, positive frame of mind. But I was uneasy from the beginning due to a very brief exchange with Harold as the others were still finding their seats. He had asked if he could sit in the chair beside me stating: "I need to sit next to a woman so I can stay awake." I knew he was being flirtatious and had some discomfort with that. Additionally, I was concerned about his declaration that he was bored – I thought that he was reneging on his commitment to the group.

The mood in the room quickly moved off Amy's pride when Kathy quietly said how uncomfortable she was with last week. She said sadly "We're born with a handicap of some kind." Kathy was a quite a depressed woman and had seemed resigned to the fact that her life would never get much better. I asked Kathy to describe the feelings associated with being uncomfortable when Amy interjected with a somber description of how she thought the group was feeling: "Last time we talked, I tried to forget about it and start a new day being happy. If we bring it up a second time, then we'll go deeper. I'd hold my breath wondering if we'd come to a solution so that we don't become upset all the time. How're we going to feel when we go back out?" I was very moved by her thoughtful and descriptive synopsis and noted that I had rarely heard anyone, staff or client, describe their experience with such fluidity.

I was so absorbed by Amy's eloquence that I had not noticed Harold brooding. Apparently Jesse had, and asked for his comments about Amy's feelings. Harold was particularly disinterested, sullen, and even surly. There was an anger and resentment in his voice when he answered with "I dunno," keeping his hand down and eyes focused on his headphone wires. Jesse persisted: "How're you now?" Still Harold refused to participate: "No one will understand. I'm thinking about whether this is the right place for me, that's all." I took his comments personally, wondering if we had failed to meet his needs, and then quickly thought that perhaps this was another of Harold's narcissistic ploys to ensure our concern revolved around him. Before there was any opportunity to ponder further, Harold began his attack: "Sometimes, I find this boring. AA meetings were better. What's best for me is not best for you. I wouldn't be here except that my counselor keeps telling me that I should. I thought we'd be talking about drugs, alcohol, or sexuality problems here. When I hear the others' problems, I get more depressed. Like Maureen, she makes me depressed and Mark doesn't say anything. And this one (pointing to Len) hardly says anything. One's the ringmaster, the other one's the puppet." Harold then turned to Amy as though to ensure that she was also the recipient of his pejorative comments: "It's not important to me what I wear, or what I look like. Jesse and Jenny wear what they like, they don't make a big issue of it." Amy looked crushed, as did the others, and I immediately tried to rescue her from having to provide a defense for herself and turned to Harold with admonishment: "When you're dissatisfied with yourself, you find fault with everyone else to avoid looking at yourself. It's up to you whether you want to be here or not, no one is forcing you. Your feedback wasn't helpful, it was critical." Jesse tried to rein Harold in as well: "You dropped a bombshell. You went around the room and said nasty things to the others. You trivialized the group. Your assessment of people in the group was unfair."

Later, as we debriefed we admitted our fears that in spite of some efforts, the damage had been done, our interventions were too little, too late – Harold had succeeded in dismantling the group and wounding its members. When Dr. Shapero asked us the next day "Did either of you stop him, interrupt him and say 'That's enough'," I winced inside. I had to admit that I did not have the insight or the confidence to do so at the time and agreed that I had been remiss by not intervening earlier. I had also felt that the group needed to respond to Harold so as to enhance their individual growth but, in hindsight, I knew it had been far too dangerous a risk.

Throughout the next session, I was furious with Harold and found my voice becoming stern as I tried hard to wrestle his unbridled ego back in place. I was heartened as each one of the other group members took Harold to task and asserted them-selves in a way that I had not thought possible. Their anger and indignation was visibly intense – Harold backed away, concerned that he was being perceived as a "jerk". He showed little remorse to the others and left as incorrigible as he had arrived: "If you think of me as a jerk, go ahead. I'm sick of being nice to people."

Even Amy's quiet weeping had no effect; Harold could not hide his rancor, and vehemently denied Jesse's observation that how we behave in the group is reflective of how we behave in the "real" world. Jesse said that Harold had revealed himself and there was no denying. That insight was particularly infuriating to Harold, and seemed to anger him more than anything else that had been said. Jesse and I both had our doubts about whether he should continue in the group and whether he could be helped. We realized that Harold had the capacity to immolate the group process for the sake of his pride and that we could therefore never let down our guard with him again. Our strategy was to talk to him privately before the next session and relay our determination to halt any future corrosive lambasting.

"Why don't you give him a chance to say something first?" Dr. Shapero advised us before the next session began; it was a change from his previous position and I felt quite relieved to hear this new strategic maneuver. Jesse and I were both very nervous about what we would face that day – was Harold even going to show and, if he did, were the others going to come. Our biggest fear was that he would not display an ounce of remorse, and everyone would disband. So with great trepidation, mixed with a determination that he not get the better of us again, we opened the session by asking Harold to speak. I noted that he looked contrite, somewhat pale and this time had very good eye contact with me. "I'm feeling miserable and bad. I asked myself all week, 'Why did I do that?' It was my grandfather's death, I couldn't talk about it so I took it out on the others here. I'd like to apologize to the group. I wonder if they understand where I'm coming from because now, I could use some friends and comfort." There was a long pause, none of the others group members seemed particularly moved by the explanation of the grandfather's death, and like me, they probably had their doubts that it was true. I asked the group how they were feeling and whether or not they were prepared to accept Harold's apology. Slowly, one by one they acknowledged him with an "I do" until it was Andrew's turn: "I do, but I'm still upset." Again, there was a long silence as they were each contemplating whether to take the risk to say more – how would we move ahead with this kind of tension?

I knew that it would be important to frame Harold's outburst last week in a way that would encourage him to stay in the group, and also to provide the others with a glimpse of his real issues. I turned to him, and as I spoke he gazed back intently: "Now we know why you're in the group, Harold. You badly need to work on your tendency to destroy relationships. What are you going to do about it?" It was the first time that I had confronted him with such confidence; because he trivialized the role of women, and had been so flirtatious, Jesse and I had decided that I would deliver the first challenge. Harold tried to dart past me a few times: "I don't know." I kept on: "Your behavior causes a lot of pain to yourself and others. What approach are you going to take?" Again, resistance: "I don't know. I haven't thought much about it." I toned down my intensity ever so slightly and tried again: "It would be helpful to hear what you're going to do about it." Finally, Harold relented and admitted that he would have to think before he spoke: "My problem is that I don't think." I added: "When you're angry, you dump on other people." Jesse jumped in to ensure that no one doubted we were excusing Harold's actions on the basis of a bad mood. He said to Harold: "It's not just that you weren't yourself last week. This has happened before in your life." Harold tried to get off the hot seat and attract Len's attention by softly lamenting that he knew Len would never want to be his friend ever again. But, surprisingly, considering how hurt she had been last week, it was Amy who jumped in to reassure Harold: "You still have a friend in me. It still bothers me a bit though." Amy's conciliatory gesture rekindled the anger that the others were obviously sitting on. Len challenged her: "But how could you still be friends after what happened? Aren't you worried that it could happen again, and again, and then what?" Amy admitted that she had been quite worried and afraid that Harold would never speak to her again. Then she added innocently, "Well if it happened again, then the question would be 'Who died?'" to which I smiled – I was not sure if she was being facetious or not, but it certainly was an effective retort to Len.

As the session continued, we moved on to the topic of death as one of the women's boyfriends was dying of Alzheimer's disease and she shared with the group how painful it would be to have to move him to a nursing home. Several other members offered stories about deaths of individuals that were close to them as well. As the discussion on this topic was wrapping up, Amy interjected with a startling insight about Harold: "These are really interesting stories. If we go back to last week, Harold was talking about his grandfather's death and putting us down. But today, other people are talking about death, but they're not putting us down. I've suddenly got it now." She laughed lightly, threw her arms up as we so often do with a eureka experience and seemed satisfied that she had found a way to reason with Harold's apology, and at the same time give credence to her disappointment with him. Harold sat silently. I knew that this session had been an extremely important transition of re-entry into the group and was proud of how honestly and graciously the others had dealt with him. Throughout the next session Harold had worked hard to interject and provide what he perceived to be supportive comments when the others spoke. With reasonable caution, they patiently tolerated his questioning and even obsequious concern at times. I wondered if Harold realized that he was no longer seen as the superior participant, the smartest, best looking, most capable member – now the others had much to pity in him and his position of leader was now open to the next interested candidate.

I sat back in my chair chagrined and somewhat amused when Harold's workshop counselor left a message a few days later that his grandfather had died over a year ago. I had called her out of curiosity and with some concern that our decision to not address this with Harold was the right thing to do. I wondered if he thought we had bought the story and was struck not so much by the lie, but in his determination to stay in the group – clearly it was worth a lot to him. I discussed with Dr. Shapero the whole issue of the dead grandfather story and he advised that we confront Harold with it privately before the next group.

Harold usually arrived earlier for the sessions and, predictably, he was waiting outside the room with the other group members playing with his headphone wires. I motioned to him from across the lobby to follow me, trying to spare him undue embarrassment by approaching him in a more visible manner. He looked very nervous, followed me to the stairs and then refused to go any further: "Am I in trouble? Because if I am, I'm not coming." I replied that we needed to speak to him and after going back and forth like this a few more times, he reluctantly followed. Jesse was waiting for us in a small conference room. I began by telling Harold that I telephoned his worker to find out if he was all right due to his grandfather's death, only to be told that the death had occurred quite some time ago. "When exactly did your grandfather die?" I questioned. Harold did not flinch and comfortably replied "About a year ago." I added: "Then what were you thinking by telling the group last week that he had just died?" He replied "I'm not over his death, I was thinking about it during the group." It went exactly as Dr. Shapero had predicted – Harold would use the anniversary of the death as an excuse. We made it clear to Harold that he would have to inform the other group members of the truth. I looked at Harold hard with a knowing expression and said: "I think you know what we mean." That seemed to draw his attention from the game-playing: "Are you saying I'm a con artist?" We did not answer back. Harold tentatively walked toward the room where the group was waiting for us to begin.

The group started with a general discussion about how often we say we are feeling "fine" when we are not. Several of the members exchanged some very honest and meaningful dialogue about why this phenomenon occurs even within the group. I focused on one of the women who had avoided confronting Harold two weeks previously, hoping to help her, and at the same time cue Harold to speak, but he continued to stare at the floor silently. "Friends I can trust. Jesse and Jenny I can trust. But the number one person to trust is yourself." It was the first time that Harold had spoken in the hour and I wondered if he was gearing up to confess, since we were on the right topic. Jesse skillfully slipped in: "Trust is a very important topic that sometimes leads to betrayal." Harold picked up the cue and turned to Jesse: "Is it time to be honest?" Jesse replied with a simple "Yes." Harold began: "It may come as a shock to you guys. It's been six months since my grandfather died. It feels like just yesterday. Sorry to put you on the spot." I shot a look over to Jesse knowing that one of us would have to confront the latest lie. The group also seemed shocked, exactly as Harold predicted they would be, and there were several minutes of silence. Then, the others began to throw angry questions at Harold, who was desperate to appease them in some way: "I had a hard time getting over his death." I jumped in with the unpleasant task of having to embarrass him yet again: "Harold, try again. You've described something different to what you told us before the group began." He shot back: "I don't remember." Jesse retorted: "I remember and believe that you remember as well." Eventually, Harold corrected his second story and admitted that death had occurred 12 months ago.

Amy came to Harold's defense, like she had in the past: "Isn't that why we're here, to share feelings. If I say something to you and then give a totally different story, when I have time to think it over, then I remember." Jesse challenged her: "Sometimes we're confused, but sometimes, we get caught in a lie." As so often happened, Amy then offered further insight which applied specifically to Harold, but without speaking directly to him: "You know they are a liar when they don't look in your eyes." Amy continued to receive encouragement from Jesse and the other group members to look Harold in the eye and tell him what she thought, however, she backed down, disappointed and seemingly hurt: "I just never thought I would hear that word here – liar." She put her hands up to her head as though trying to forget the whole incident. Ironically, Harold decided to talk: "I lied because I wanted you guys to like me again after I said all those bad things to you." Harold continued to unfold the problem in a larger context: "I have a bad habit of lying. I've heard it from my father and my girl-friend. Everybody has talked to me about it."

As Harold relayed more of his negative habits, the others became more incensed; Harold turned on them in anger having had enough of their feedback: "I've got friends in the real world even if I don't here. I made a *big* mistake all right – coming to this group." Although Jesse and I tried various encouraging comments, the greatest wisdom offered to Harold came from Peter who had been listening intently throughout. With heartfelt compassion, he turned to Harold: "Give yourself another week. It's better not to just give up on the group. Try new things. It's better to talk about the feedback." I was moved to tears by Peter, a blind man who had many years institutionalized, with no family, a man who lived alone. How fitting that such sound advice came from him. He continued: "Give yourself another chance. Don't quit the group." Jesse turned to Peter: "I really liked what you said because it shows that we want Harold here. Peter, you've had a tough life and with your difficulties, well it's your perseverance and strength, it is something that we can all learn from." Peter's "Thank you" was full of emotion. What a wonderful finish to a tough session. I noted that when the group had officially ended, Harold looked at me and said he would be back next week as though nothing had happened.

Harold did come the following week, however, it turned out to be his last session. We had strategized that during the session it would be important to curb Harold's story-telling and instead encourage him to talk more about his feelings. His stories would often go on and on in detail which diverted the whole group from interacting with each other and prevented more meaningful exchanges from occurring. Harold's "speeches" on the various incidents and relationships that he shared about his life character-istically revealed only a paucity of emotional content.

When Peter was encouraged to talk about his loneliness and then began to describe his troubled relationship with his parents, Harold jumped in with quick advice: "I have something. When you said your parents don't care, I'm sure your parents are nice, they're just too caught up in what they're doing, too busy. Sure, they care about you." Peter was frustrated at the lack of empathy and a stranger's defense of family members who had caused him a lot of pain. He firmly retorted: "I don't think my parents do. They don't call, write, or ever see me. I have to call them. I have bad memories of visiting them at Christmas. It's a bad feeling. I don't want to go there." I was pleased that Harold listened and offered an empathic response in return: "Yes, it is a bad feeling, especially at Christmas." Harold continued to interject here and there with advices that he thought would help Peter and re-establish some position of importance with all of us. He got into a debate with another participant about whether or not revenge was a worthwhile response for Peter to act on and was so caught up in that power struggle that the heart of the issue was momentarily lost.

The last thing that Harold said to all of us at the end of the session was "Sometimes I do bad things to my mom," to which I had to respond: "Sorry we're out of time." Regretfully, I never saw Harold again. He called before each of the next two sessions with some excuse that led all of us to suspect that he wanted out. I decided to call him and see what he would say about the next meeting. He told me that he would come if he "had nothing better to do" to which I encouraged him to tell me what was really going on. He admitted that he did not want to attend anymore and felt that he was not getting enough out of it. I had just been reading in Yalom's *The Theory and Practice of Group Psychotherapy* that "an inexperienced therapist is particularly threatened by the patient who threatens to drop out. You begin to fear that, one by one, your patients will leave and that you will one day come to the group and find that you (and perhaps a co-therapist) are the only ones there" (Yalom 1970, p.322). It was all true to my feelings and I felt quite depressed about the success of the project when I hung up the phone.

I had begun to question the efficacy of group psychotherapy for the developmentally disabled and had admitted it openly in the last supervision session, much to the dismay of all. It was not just Harold's quitting that prompted it; some of the others also appeared to be struggling and, like Harold, two other participants had quit from another group. The political tension was also mounting. While many of the direct care staff appeared somewhat satisfied with the work that we were doing, a number of management personnel were less than supportive. One, in particular, had even complained about our use of the room and the fact that the tables were no longer arranged as he would have liked. I was also having my doubts as to whether we could sustain the enthusiasm and interest of the group leaders, some of whom were finding the supervision sessions quite tough as they struggled to improve their quality of delivery.

Surprisingly, the group was relieved at Harold's departure and their determination to move on gave me hope that we would not eventually lose all of them. Before I announced that Harold would definitely not be returning, Len asked where he was and when he got his answer, replied: "I'm angry and now I can't finish my anger with him. I'm angry about how rude he was to us and how he lied. I'm sorry to say, I'm happy that he's gone." Andrew also jumped in: "I was mad too. I'm glad he left." The others had less harsh words and even lamented that they would miss his ability to give feedback. Like myself, Len also felt more insecure about the foundation of the group with Harold's abandonment: "It leaves me in the middle, kind of hanging on a loose rope. I feel like the group will continue, but I don't feel secure 'cause people are disappearing." Peter added: "In mid air!" We all felt reassured by the idea that two new members were due to join the group fairly soon.

It was clear that the group wanted to move on and heal from Harold's presence *and* absence – both had negatively impacted. I thought that Len captured the reason for Harold's disappearance best: "He put on an act at first and then showed us his true colors. When he couldn't get away with it, he left."

Todd – Sad
without Tears

When I first met Todd, I was instantly charmed by his friendly, frank and somewhat naïve conversation. He seemed on first glance to be someone ideal to work with as he had lots of colorful stories to share about his life and was intensely committed to forming relationships that would enhance his happiness, whether with staff or peers. Todd had already been in group counseling with us as a participant in a pilot project in the spring of 1997 when we invited him to join our next group therapy venture. He was considered the most endearing and interesting participant by the observers and the two group leaders. Todd demonstrated a level of complexity and sensitivity that surpassed any other group member. Most of the time Todd was fascinating to watch and left me feeling full of emotion after many sessions – close to tears more often than I imagined would occur in my work setting. I was not what I considered to be a sentimental person and it was rare that I ever shed a tear at work as the professional code was a powerful force throughout the agency; although we were continually interacting with people whose lives had a strong element of tragedy, neither sadness nor sorrow were considered helpful, and were generally regarded as unacceptable responses. Professionalism characterized by control of one's emotions is a common standard in many social work positions. I eventually came to realize that a code of professionalism should not be one that requires staff to withhold emotion, but rather one that encourages the acknowledgement of emotion. It is the denial of one's feelings, however strongly positive or negative, that leads to untold abuses within the field; often, this abuse takes the form of unnecessary control and domination of the client as a means of coping with the excess of emotion that begins to surface in the social worker or caregiver.

Todd's life story was just as tragic as many others that I have worked with, but his poignant descriptions and malapropisms were particularly touching. I remember fondly when I first heard Todd announce that he had a serious gambling problem and was considering going to "gamblers monopolous". One was left with the urge to both laugh and cry and I often thought that Todd knew there was a strong element of humor in his presentation that he enjoyed as well. Todd could be as endearing as he was frustrating with his obstinate need to persist with issues: his counselor's failure to show or lack of support, fighting with his girlfriend, or no one to help him get a job. Watching Todd in his newly assigned group as an observer was a different experience for me, as previously I had been in the position of one of his group leaders. I felt a little protective of him although he had no trouble finding his place in the group. My feelings had more to do with a strong identification with the tremendous pain that he had experienced in life and overcome, and his ability to use humor in a somewhat naïve manner. Todd was also quite willing to verbally share his perspective on life even when it was unsolicited, eager to ensure that he was part of the process.

One of the group leaders early on in the group complimented once: "Todd, you're a survivor" and although he asked her "What does that mean?", I sensed that he knew exactly what she meant. Todd had been sent to a large institution for persons with developmental disabilities when he was just nine years old because his family felt that they could not manage him. By his own admission, he was violent at times as a child and described an incident whereupon he threw hot tea at his father. Todd remained at the institution until he was about 30. The horrors of his life there, including both emotional and physical abuse, the perceived rejection of his family, and post-institution discharge, were a part of Todd that we never fully got to in the last group he was invited to participate in. I was hoping that in this new group (which I observed weekly) the leaders would slowly uncover the layers of anger, pain, shame, rejection, and fear that I sensed tormented Todd. He had regular altercations in the community, whether it was with bus drivers, cashiers in grocery stores, or just strangers on the street. By his own admission, Todd described a time when he had been standing in line at a grocery store and started yelling at the cashier because he somehow felt singled out, that she was preventing him from getting through the line. Eventually the store manager was called in to deal with the cacophonous outcry. Todd also had ongoing battles with his support staff and complained that he was chronically late and was not helping him get a job, to name a few in a long list of issues. This particular worker was someone I knew well and had hung in with Todd for over ten years. He caught a lot of Todd's anger and found him frustrating, however, when offered to transfer him to another worker he smiled and said "No, I think I'll keep him, he seems to be improving." I understood his sentiments as I found Todd to be quite charming, and while he was extremely trying at times, he was fascinating to observe and interact with. He had a way of inducing guilt at the thought of any of us "abandoning" him – it seemed to be his greatest fear.

Throughout the beginning sessions Todd demanded that definitions of words be explained, claiming not to understand, perhaps as a way to challenge the leaders' competence. I often wondered though how much of his confusion was deliberately cunning and clever, innocent, naïve, or simply genuine misunderstanding. He was clearly very street smart and had survived egregious treatment and circumstances, so his lack of familiarity with certain words such as "feedback" was puzzling. It also became incredibly irritating as it was constantly interjected, seemingly just at the moment when a flow had started to happen in the group, when one of the more reticent members had finally mustered the courage to share. He forced the group leaders to work hard and at the same time gave them many valuable themes to pursue such as how it felt to be labeled "retarded". It was extremely rare for staff, never mind clients, to broach this topic and we all felt a degree of discomfort when it came to the forefront of the discussion. Todd was someone who enjoyed engaging others, so when fellow participants were struggling with a way to express themselves, he was more than happy to comment and come to their assistance in whatever way he could. He seemed to enjoy challenging Lana, one of the group leaders, perhaps because she had some slight physical resemblance to his girlfriend, Lucy, whom he fought with constantly yet clearly loved. Todd and Lucy had been a couple for many years before staff agreed that it would be acceptable for them to live together. We were well aware of how hard Todd had fought for this "privilege" and agreed to have Lucy attend one of our other groups. Todd appeared to really admire Alex, the other leader, and skillfully wrestled away his attention from other group members on numerous occasions. Alex was tolerant, kind, and determined to connect with Todd in a way that was genuine and I hope devoid of patronizing niceties.

When Mary Ann burst into tears unexpectedly in the first session over an aunt who had recently died, Todd responded with ease and warmth that even the group leaders struggled to match. He pulled out a rather dirty looking tissue from his pocket and handed it to her saying "I know how you're feeling. My father died in 1990." He continued to focus his attention on her for the entire time that she talked about it and was quite comfortable assuming a kind of big brother role. I had no doubt that Todd could show altruistic feelings and that his ability to empathize with others seemed genuine. But I was not sure whether Todd's need to monopolize certain sessions was reflective of the deep pain that he experienced or his desire to be at the center and dominate the others as a way of gaining control – something he had rarely experienced in his childhood or adult life.

Regardless, Todd was particularly central in one of the sessions in which a problem between three participants was being exposed. It was noteworthy that Todd repeatedly interjected "But I wasn't here last week" when the leaders were giving the three participants an opportunity to sort out the problem. It was true that Todd had missed the previous week and at that time the threesome problem had first been discussed; however, it seemed that it was difficult for Todd to put aside his own need to be involved in the altercation and to allow the others a significant amount of time in the session. The pattern of interjecting when others were speaking continued throughout the hour and was particularly problematic when one of the shyer women described her embarrassment about feeling in the spotlight. It was a poignant moment and clearly a difficult one for her. Paradoxically, Tom displayed little sensitivity about her situation even though this was the same woman to whom he had offered consolation in the first session. He stole the topic as well, and began to describe his own difficulty with anger: "I feel it's easier to talk about with two people. I get my anger out with one-on-one. That's the way I like it." Marsha retreated out of the discussion altogether and seemed resigned to his successful attempts to regain the leader's attention. I felt angry with Todd for being so narcissistic when he turned to Marsha and said, "I just wanted to say you're pretty." I knew he did not mean it in a flirtatious way, as Todd was quite devoted to his live-in girlfriend of five years. I thought rather that he was genuinely showing sensitivity to his treatment of her by complimenting her looks; this was a particularly difficult topic for Marsha as she had shared with the group previously how unattractive she felt. Physical appearance was another topic that was rarely discussed between staff and client despite the fact that many of the people we worked with were acutely self-conscious. We were always encouraged to accentuate the positive appearance attributes without probing what it felt like to be so obviously different and for some, quite unattractive due to varying degrees of physical deformity.

Just when I felt that he had redeemed himself, Todd rambled on again: "I put myself down every single day. Sometimes I go to the washroom and say 'That's an ugly face'." The group leaders were clearly struggling – on the one hand Todd had brought the focus of the group to himself and on the other hand it was such an important topic for everyone there. The rest of the group was not quite ready to deal with feelings of self-deprecation, although Todd persisted even after the group ended and approached Lana: "Do you ever put yourself down?" She was left somewhat speechless and muttered something about the fact that the group was over, that it would have to wait. While it seemed the most appropriate answer at the time, I couldn't help but wonder when Todd would be open like that again. I left the session with such a mixed reaction as so typically seemed to happen when observing Todd. Clearly, he had a lot to offer the others because of his willingness to expose them to their own pain and by daring to talk about their disabilities. I wondered though, could he do this without eventually robbing the others of their time?

Within a few minutes of starting, one of the more introspective group members, Nancy, asked a profound question: "Are any of us going to learn here?" Todd jumped in with alacrity and responded: "I've already learned a lot. That's why I'm in a good mood." Little did Todd know what was to come in this session and that the feedback he was about to receive would be very difficult. As usual, Todd began interjecting with numerous comments as the two leaders tried to give the floor to Nancy and provide the opportunity for her to share her concerns. He reverted to his old favorite, asking a question about the meaning of a word – this time it was "overwhelmed". Lana was ready for Todd and quipped back: "Todd, it seems sometimes that when someone is getting attention, or support, you're not sure about the meaning of a word." Todd would not back down and adamantly maintained his innocence: "I don't know. No, it's not true that I know that word." Lana moved the discussion back to Nancy and eventually on to the other participants. Todd's next intervention was to interrupt

Alex who was expending great energy trying to get two of the men who seemed disinterested to converse with one another. He blurted out "Can I ask a question?" In spite of Alex's look of annoyance, Todd continued with a series of survey-type questions (What are we going to do today? How long will it be till we break?). Alex quietly, but sternly, said: "It feels like an interruption." To make matters worse for Todd, Nancy, like the group leaders, felt that he needed to be corrected as well and challenged him in yet another way – this time, for being off topic. Poor Todd, I thought; I wonder how much longer he is going to withstand this. While I felt the feedback was valid, it began to take on a punitive tone and the straw that broke the camel's back came in the last ten minutes of the session when Todd was corrected for laughing at Nancy's joke when someone else was speaking. He was clearly defeated and discouraged when a final correction was delivered by the group leaders and muttered sarcastically "Sorry for living." He then went on with a more serious message: "Maybe this isn't the group for me. I'm not getting anything out of it." The session ended shortly thereafter, and Todd began to apologize to anyone he could, both group leaders and then the observers. I felt a mix of compassion and confusion when he looked straight at me with a pained expression: "Sorry, Jenny."

We had a long discussion about what had transpired during our group supervision with Dr. Shapero, the supervising psychologist, who expressed his concern that Todd had been too harshly dealt with and felt that perhaps he himself was partly to blame. Prior to the session, Dr. Shapero had advised both of the leaders that they needed to confront Todd, and that he had been given too much rein. We all had to agree that Alex and Lana seemed to be running behind Todd much of the time, and rarely assumed a position in which he was guided by their lead. Being novice and eager to follow Dr. Shapero's advice, both Alex and Lana, in their effort to please and attempt to do the most astute therapeutic intervention, had indeed turned up the heat too high. Still, Todd needed correction and I empathized with their dilemma. He could be so persistently central to the process and at the same time find logical ways to deflect feedback in the areas most pertinent to him.

The next week, Todd was acutely sensitive to what the group leaders were looking for and to the needs of the group in a way that I thought reflected some thoughtful resolutions on his part. Marsha was a group member who had stayed back for quite some time, reticent, she said, about being able to trust the group members. Todd helped to facilitate her misgivings: "Maybe this isn't the right group for you. Maybe one-to-one would be better." He was quickly challenged by the group leaders on this suggestion and backed off nervously; he turned to Marsha again: "Don't worry, we all like you in this group." I admired Todd's repeated efforts to keep the discussion going and to try to help Marsha resolve the issue of trust. I could see, though, that he was nervously repentant with both Lana and Alex. He was quick to apologize by hanging his head with a "sorry" about any move he made. I wondered if he was going to play any important role in the group during this session or if he felt his only purpose was to re-establish some ground as a somewhat compliant and receptive member. But the issue of trust was one that hit close to home for Todd, as well as it did for Marsha, and when the discussion got on to the topic of whether or not to trust the group leaders, Todd adamantly interjected that he did not trust his worker or the leaders only "people I know really well". He re-thought his position: "I don't even trust my own girlfriend." The discussion continued to unfold many layers of mistrust for Todd and other group members. He announced with sadness and confusion: "Maybe I don't trust anybody. I trust nobody." It struck me that Todd had survived as well as he had because he had not trusted. I tried to imagine the number of staff who had come in and out of his life, some of whom Todd had alluded to as abusive. Persons with developmental disabilities are required to place an inordinate amount of trust in those who are responsible for their care and are vulnerable to having that trust dissolve quickly and irrevocably. No one is to blame, rather, many staff can commit only to superficial relationships due to the nature of the difficulty of the work and the fact that there is such a high turnover in the field of developmental disabilities.

Todd was relentless in his determination to continue to unfold how little trust there really was in his life. He eventually hit bottom when he announced, "I don't even trust my best friend or myself," triggering an indignant reaction from one of the more withdrawn group members. Richard nearly leapt out of his chair and pointed his finger firmly in Todd's direction, "Alex!" he cried out, "He put himself down. That's a big mistake. Don't you feel ashamed of yourself?" Todd seemed startled, as were the rest of us observing, and quickly offered an olive branch: "I'm going to take your advice Richard, to try to trust people." It seemed that Todd had yet again uncovered a deep-seated fear we all face at one time or another – the ability to trust in ourselves. Alex decided to pursue Todd's self-deprecatory comments and gently asked, "Why do you put yourself down?" Todd replied with despair: "I'm stupid, I'm dumb. I've nothing to live for. I don't know why, but I do it." Now both Richard and Neil appeared mortified by Todd's words and continued desperately to try to get him to retract his comments. It appeared as though they had a fear of leaving them hanging in the air because there was unspoken understanding that others in the room had similar feelings. Richard added: "You're hurting yourself inside. You should think before you talk." Neil jumped in while shaking his head pensively: "That's putting yourself right down to the ground." The room became silent as we wondered what would happen next, would Todd back off or would the others join him in an admission that all of them must have felt at one time, the feeling of being more intellectually inadequate than the normal population. Again, this was not a subject that staff were accustomed to discussing, as it was considered too painful for any of the clients to bear and many believed they did not have the capacity to be self-reflective in this way.

Neil soon revealed why Todd's words were so difficult to hear when, shortly after Todd's admission, he began to slowly but determinedly reveal his past: "The things I've been through." Todd desperately tried to connect with Neil "I know how you feel." Neil seemed angry by the response. "Nobody in this group has been through what I've been through. Getting beatin' up all the time, abused by parents and relatives." Todd looked astonished and shook his finger fiercely "*That*, I wasn't." Neil hung his head, held his hand over his eyes and began to weep as the group watched in silence. The silence was broken when Todd asked Neil if he could get him some cold water or a tissue – he seemed desperate to console. It was one of the few times I had seen Todd squirm to get out from under the tension in the group and he asked Alex if the session could be stopped. When that strategy did not work, he added several times that he knew what Neil was going through although Todd steered the topic to talking about the loss of his father. Either Todd was relating to the notion of pain in general or there had been abusive memories in his past that, while deeply buried, were slowly surfacing when Neil acknowledged his. It did not seem the right time to delve into this as the group members were reeling from Neil's dialogue. The leaders also wanted to afford the group members the opportunity to take care of each other at that moment rather than deferring to staff as was so typically the case. I was touched by Todd's parting philosophy and thought how often I had felt the same way that he did: "Life must go on, I think."

Christmas was just around the corner and the group members expressed mixed feelings about the holiday, especially Todd. He appeared to have been in a less serious mood during the session until he was asked "Do you see your family over the holidays?" His first reply was a resolute "Nope" that left little room for exploration. I wondered if he was tired of thinking about that topic and had been asked too many times over the years. The staff in group homes worked especially hard to reunite family members with the residents, often feeling like peacemakers and advocates as they tried to convince reticent siblings, cousins, and even parents to share their holiday. He continued on, though: "How can I see them? My father's not alive, my sisters aren't in town. I don't care where my brother lives, I hate to say it. They never phone me, but

I still love my family." I listened intently to Todd's comments, wondering if he felt he had to say that he loved them even if he felt unloved. When Todd went further to isolate the real issue as he saw it, the group responded with silence – they were difficult words for all of us to hear. "I wish my mom and sister would invite me up, they don't want me. Maybe because of my handicap?" Todd shrugged his shoulders as he spoke and continued: "I don't know, I've never asked them. I'll phone them tonight and find out. I never see them, never. That's the honest truth." I noted that when the group dealt with the issue of disability, that it was usually Todd who initiated it; I admired his courage and his willingness to show the others how vulnerable he felt. I wondered how it was that he coped so well while carrying such pained feelings of rejection. He eventually brought up his father, as so often happened in the group, but this time described his loss in a way that we had not heard before – as the dead link to the family. "I wish my father was still alive. I didn't want him to die. He's the only one who came to Maddock [the institution], he came. When he was alive, then I used to see them at Christmas." It was clear that Todd felt some responsibility for the family's alienation and the shame he believed to have caused them. He took the blame of his isolation from them: "I'm the only handicapped in my family. I feel dumb, stupid, ugly, nothing. I can't read or write." It certainly was not the first time that the others had heard Tom's recapitulation of his essential being in such plaintive terms. I felt compassionate and at the same time concerned as to how the leaders could bridge an ideal of hope to all that despair. Todd did not allow much room for pity, and seemed to be comparing his coping strategies to Neil's from the previous week. Specifically, he made reference to the fact that he was not crying about it: "There's nothing to cry about or laugh about." Todd's verbal display of pride surprised me as he had so tenderly accepted the others' tears when they were distressed; perhaps it was something for him to feel good about, that he could face those feelings with prowess, desolate as they were.

Todd had, by now, captivated the group leaders and although they both indirectly comforted Neil, who was quietly crying, by assuring Todd that crying was healthy, Todd paid little attention. He showed little awareness of the fact that his last comments were both pejorative and insightful. He went on to describe a particularly cruel story of childhood, one that I heard from him before, yet still was deeply moved. "My dad told me to get my sister Betty. I went to the neighbor's house and knocked on the door, but there was no answer. I sat on the porch not knowing what to do. My neighbor came out and whacked me on the head with a broom. She thought I was a burglar. The doctor said I came within this much [gestured with his thumb and finger] of surviving. I asked my mom, 'Is this why I'm handicapped?' But I was born like this, that wasn't the reason." There was much more to this story for Todd than the abusive reaction of a neighbor; he seemed equally distressed that no one would believe it was true. He questioned the leaders' position, and even gestured over to the observers as well, eventually insisting that if he had to, he would call his mother long distance to vindicate himself, to prove his truthfulness. "It doesn't matter who I tell, they all think I'm lying," Todd repeated a few times. Eventually, he appeared less interested in whether he was believed and returned back to theme of crying to which Neil graciously replied: "It's good to get it out though Todd." In the last few minutes of the session, Todd tried to retract his position that crying was not the bravest response and I was interested in how easy it was for him to apologize: "Sorry, Neil, I'm sad without tears, and you're sad with tears. Nothing against you Neil." It was this type of consideration, the willingness to rectify by way of apology, that was so generous about Todd, and that heightened his impact and importance in the group. He beautifully captured the dilemma of so many people with developmental disabilities; their sadness, fears, anger, joy must all be tempered, tacitly harbored, so as not to disrupt the equilibrium that staff and family try so hard to maintain. Extremes of emotions are often considered a problem, throwing the individual off-balance from the bridge that we all attempt to secure, to ensure normalizing progress is made.

Todd was one of the first to comment on Richard's arm resting behind Suzanne and how closely he was sitting with her at the beginning of one of the sessions. "If she's his girlfriend, I guess that's his business." But clearly, everyone was uncomfortable in the group and both Richard and Suzanne had violated one of the few rules that had been spelled out at the first session – no relationships of an intimate nature between group members. Dr. Shapero had been adamant that this was an uncompromising rule and explained to all of us in detail how the formation of a couple in a group disrupts all dynamics such that the group loses its cohesiveness. I remember he said it was highly unlikely, however, having only occurred once in 30 years of his group therapy experience. Todd was the first to get clarification from Richard and Suzanne when he asked them point blank: "Are you a couple?" When he got his confirmation from Suzanne, Todd was nervous, having remembered the words of the group leaders and muttered: "Anyway, I don't want to upset them two." It prompted Todd to talk about his own relationship and he openly declared their tumultuous patterns: "We fight everywhere, but we still love each other. I know what the problem is, I'm spoiling her. I gave her a watch, clothes, and she doesn't give me anything. We argue and fight at home. We might get thrown out of the building." I thought about how transparent Todd appeared to be and upon closer examination, his complexity. I wondered if he was talking about his own turmoil, and devoted relationship, as a generous way to distract the group from Richard and Suzanne, or if he was becoming consumed with his own pain, as so often happened. He continued with a look of melancholy: "I love her, she loves me. I don't want to lose her."

One of the group leaders asked Todd if he felt the same about the group – that he gave more than he got. I thought it was an extremely interesting and relevant question and was impatient for his answer. But Todd avoided the question, seemingly not understanding, and pursued a slightly different direction. "I'm nice to my friends, but not to myself. Sometimes I wish I wasn't alive. I wish I was with my dad." Then he said very quietly and with what appeared to be great sincerity: "Sometimes I feel that I'm gonna end it all. I don't mean it, but I feel like it." The other participants jumped in with all sorts of suggestions for Todd, like how important it is to keep busy, but he politely denied the gentle admonishments as helpful. Perhaps, no one could stand the pain that life as a developmentally disabled person could be so unbearable as to wish it to end. As so often happened, Todd laid out his feelings for all to see, even those that were the most painful to bear, with seeming ease. I watched him, feeling a mix of admiration and understanding. His descriptions of those moments of despair, his longing for a dead father, were so brutally honest – it all made sense in understanding Todd.

Todd continued the next week but with a series of self-deprecating comments that seemed relentless: "I can't read, I can't write. I feel dumb. I care for my friends, but not myself. I've never had a paid job. I got fired from my volunteer job. It's not worth living, I have no future..." The group members rallied to try to convince him that there was some hope and that they too had their troubles, but to no avail. Not only was Todd determined to see his plight as hopeless, he refused to acknowledge that the others were also chasing happiness with little success. His forays were successful in keeping the others at a baffled and frustrated distance: "But you read and write"; "But, you had a paid job"; "No one else here lived in an institution." Unfortunately, the group leaders let Todd continue, even encouraging his painful disclosures at the expense of the feelings of the others who were clearly becoming more and more disenchanted and angry about the lack of attention. As well, they were highly agitated by Todd's admissions. Marsha's last statements to the leaders captured the frustration and anger the group was feeling about Todd's ubiquitous presence and the subsequent deference he was given: "Well, what do you two [Lana and Alex] think about us? About everybody in this room? What do you think of us, the whole person? I was born with my

handicap and will probably die with it." Her message could not
have been clearer – I was not heard today and why did you dismiss
me so resolutely.

The leaders paid for their mistakes the following week, and
dearly. Marsha relentlessly asserted her belief that the group was
not to be trusted and was unforgiving about a suggestion that the
leaders had proposed weeks earlier, to audiotape the sessions:
"You guys were gonna start audiotaping. I don't know if I can trust
you again. You might blab it out." She continued to interject her
feelings of mistrust for at least half of the hour when Todd
decided to join with her, agreeing that the participants could not
be trusted: "I agree with Marsha, there is nobody in the group that
I trust." In spite of protests from the leaders that Todd had shared
quite a lot of his feelings and, therefore, must have trusted, it was
too late – the group was in jeopardy. In fact, the whole structure of
the group began to unravel at a frightening speed as the discussion moved from a lack of trust to Marsha's fear that maybe some-
body in the group would go so far as to follow her, or assault her
physically.

Interestingly, Todd played with the idea of following the
male leader of the group: "I'm going to follow Alex home one
day." Perhaps Todd sensed Alex's fear of the topic of trust as well
and was fantasizing about a reversal of power between them.
Towards the end of the session he probed Alex to find out how he
would feel if Lana followed him. It was a curious idea and I suspected that Todd was hoping to both capture Alex's imagination
and was perhaps curious about Alex's fears of being pursued. It
was so rare to see a client putting one of the staff on the hot seat,
and I couldn't help but admire Todd's boldness.

The group leaders struggled in their effort to confront Todd
the next time they saw him, after the Christmas break. He was
bored and uninterested with the structure of reviewing goals for
the New Year. It was a banal topic to someone who had probably
been asked to review goals on a regular basis. Todd began to crack
his knuckles, paying no heed to the gentle suggestions that the
noise was distracting. By the time it was Todd's turn to reiterate

his goals, he was either so bored or frustrated that he denied ever having had a problem with anger: "I don't get mad that much. I haven't been yelling, but my girlfriend has. She needs a good psychiatrist." Todd continued to crack his knuckles right through to the end with no effective objection from the leaders; he seemed to be escaping them.

Upon reviewing the "knuckle-cracking" session, we all saw some humor in it, irritating as it was. I also thought his behavior served as important feedback for the leaders – more than knuckles would be cracking if they did not strengthen the foundation of the group. The leaders were well primed to keep an eye on Todd the following week, and when he began his next tactic they were ready for him. This time he had resurrected his old favorite "What does that mean?" in response to other members' serious reflections. Todd had always pursued clarification on the definition of words, but not with such frequency and regularity; he appeared to have found a substitute to knuckle-cracking. The first one was ignored and the second one was responded with: "What do you think it means, Todd?" Fighting question with question did not work and when Todd tried his third tactic, falling asleep, he was confronted more forcefully. Todd's behavior was characterized in the group as "insensitive" to others and an inability to pay attention. Todd protested by spending the rest of the session defending his altruistic inclinations: "I like to help others, listening to them. I'd like to meet more friends and help others out." He then began to strongly protest at one of the participant's announcement that he might be moving to France and made several statements suggesting how important his presence was to the group: "You can't leave, we need you here. You're a part of this group."

Todd approached me as he was about to leave that session to tell me that his New Year's resolution was to be nice to people. Once again, his complex insights fascinated me, for on the one hand he was clearly using numerous tactics to make sure that he was noticed in the group, and on the other hand, the negative feedback appeared to genuinely disturb him. He was bothered at having been perceived as uncaring, appearing to be quite affected by this unseemly image. I wondered if Todd's frustrations were masked behind his irritating habits, like interrupting. Perhaps he was trying to convey a very important message about himself – it was difficult to feel cared for when the others had the attention and focus. On the surface a very child-like need and behavior, yet one that many adults hide from admitting.

After observing Todd in the next session, I began to realize that his inability to feel cared for was more complex than just needing a constant stream of attention. Todd did not appear to have ever experienced contentment, even momentarily, and his "one-upmanship" on the tragic stories that others told was probably his way of ensuring that he stayed miserable. After all, being miserable led to feelings of importance, captured the interest of others, and was far more enticing than anything a positive frame of mind seemed to offer. It became particularly evident during one of the sessions, when one of the quiet members of the group, Bill, revealed a sordid and sorrowful tale that he claimed was too shameful to tell anyone previously. It agitated Todd and he desperately tried to recall a life story that was just that much more tragic, full of more pathos than Bill's. Actually, he attempted three times during the hour to introduce a tale of woe, starting with an incident that had occurred in the morning, to as far back as 1984. Todd was reluctant to even describe the first story, perhaps because it had a familiar ring to all of us – persecution from the community: "I was waiting for the streetcar, but it ran by. The driver almost ran me off. Why didn't the driver wait? Boy, I was uptight about that." The second story, which came up no more than 15 minutes later, was even more personal: "Me and my girlfriend were at the Eaton Center and I was just reaching over to get some sugar when a lady yelled at me not to spill coffee on her. I'm not the kind of guy who hurts people." The group by now had developed some closeness and some of the members were very supportive of Todd's plight. Neil responded quickly: "Put it this way, she was just trying to frame you. You did the right thing to walk away from it."

The last story emerged under slightly different circumstances than the first two. When Bill confessed his painful past, and felt that he had been unfairly blamed for a crime that he did not commit, Todd was initially very inquisitive about the details and then abruptly switched topics: "I'm the only one here who doesn't live with their parents." Neil objected and reminded Todd that he also did not live with his parents. Todd responded: "Well, I never *see* my parents." Neil was not going to let it go: "Todd, I never see my parents either." When all that failed, Todd finished with what he believed to be the most tragic episode ever heard in the group: "One time in the 1980s when I was coming home from floor hockey one of my friends said something that I didn't like. Then he punched me and I said to him 'Do you want to fight?' He just walked away, but I got so mad that I put my fist through the glass at the subway station. The police came and took me to jail. Luckily, my counselor bailed me out."

Ironically, the next time we saw Todd, he calmly described to the group that earlier in the week a car had nicked him. Yet, the story did not hold much interest for him; he politely tolerated the others' concerned responses. I wondered if Todd's need for reaction to this story was minimized because the driver had apparently been extremely remorseful about the accident, and stayed with Todd for quite some time. But, it seemed that Todd was in a thoughtful frame of mind that day as he responded appropriately to the others' difficulties, offering genuine encouragement. His behavior was not just a token abnegation to the pressure from the leaders over the previous weeks to share time with the other participants; he just seemed to be in less need. He was particularly helpful with Marsha, offering her valuable suggestions about how to alleviate her loneliness while acknowledging similar feelings. This time, it did not take away from her presentation.

Todd: "I'm lonely in one way. I never see my family. That's the only way."

Marsha:	"Yeah? That's pretty difficult. I feel lonely here because I'm the only girl."
Todd:	"What have you got against guys?"
Marsha:	"I'm nervous."

There were many other exchanges like this in which Todd pursued Marsha's feelings in a way that no one, other than the leaders, was capable or interested in doing. The ability to delve into the complex was noteworthy about Todd and he surprised us all by pursuing the group leaders next: "Why don't you two [Alex and Lana] talk about your problems? You just heard ours, now what about the two of you?" Not only was it an interesting observation and question, it was bold in a courageous sense, completely lacking in contentiousness. His curiosity about the private problems of the leaders was one that all group members probably felt to varying degrees, but I thought it was more than that. Both leaders had difficulty with openness and had been participating in the group at times with a self-effacing aura that I believe Todd was reacting to, even if it was at a subconscious level. What he was really challenging was the power imbalance between staff and client. So often, in order to maintain a modicum of professionalism, staff protest that the client has the power, they are merely facilitating. In fact, it is rare that the client has the power in a system designed for service delivery and I believe that it is better to admit the existence of power differentials than to pretend none is there.

I had never seen Todd so jovial and playful as he was in the next session, although I had certainly witnessed that aspect of his personality outside of the group and had always regarded him as someone who enjoyed humor. It started out playful from the beginning when a new member objected to being referred to as a "girl"; Todd had noted the need for more "girls" in the group. He never really took her objection seriously, although backed off without offending her. The playful talk took a serious turn when surprisingly, Bill, one of the more shy members, admitted that he played a hide-and-go-seek game with his mother. Mario had a strong reaction to Bill's confession and began to comment on what he had heard. Then Alex made a connection between the way that Mario had hid in the group on an emotional level and the description of play between Bill and his mother. It was an attempt to keep the dialogue going as Bill rarely contributed. Todd captured it well: "He [Mario] came up from hibernating." It was remarkable to me how insightful his comment was – the image of Mario hibernating depicted his transformation so well. Todd decided to also respond to Bill by adding: "When I was a kid, I liked to do what adults did, believe it or not." I was curious about Todd's temptation to add to Bill's embarrassment, by emphasizing that even as a child, he had never played in such a way as to be chased by his mother. "I'm not like Bill. He plays games. I do mostly adult things." Then Neil began to laugh out loud, admitting that he found Bill's story "strange" which prompted Bill to retract the whole story: "I played games all the time at school. I don't play that often now." The three men, Bill, Mario, and Todd, continued to exchange childhood stories about play, although the tension surrounding Bill's strangeness and the mystery about his relationship with his mother were ever present.

I caught Todd winking at Richard towards the end of the session in what appeared to be a playful gesture, or perhaps a sign of camaraderie. It struck me that although I had seen Todd in playful, fun-loving moods outside the group sessions on numerous occasions, it was certainly the first time that he had been so free in the group – a sign that the participants were becoming more intimate and the leaders were more comfortable. I also attributed it to the presence of the new member, Marie, who had joined the group for the first time that week. She was a nervous woman, but ironically, had a somewhat calming effect on the others because she was so frank about her feelings, so thoughtful and considerate about not hurting anyone. Her softness and gentleness was having quite an impact on everyone. Up to the time of her joining the group, Todd had assumed the nurturing role. I was curious to observe how he would react to her in future sessions, whether he could share that role.

When Mario confronted Todd at the next session, I was shocked. As so often happened at the beginning of the group, Todd was jumping from topic to topic about how his week or day had been going and relayed a list of the latest mishaps. When Mario muttered something to Neil, Todd parroted Neil's response to speak up, although Todd did not appear invested. Mario was angry when, after repeating himself clearly, Todd admitted that he "wasn't concentrating. My mind was on something else." Mario shot back with righteous anger: "I'm not gonna explain it again. I feel bad that you weren't listening. Didn't you ask me to speak up?" When Todd continued in the same vein with Marsha, Alex focused the group on Todd's behavior, hoping to provide some insights for Todd as to why he solicited others' responses and then paid them no heed. But Todd would have no part of the exploration: "I give up, man. I made a mistake. Everybody's jumping down my back. Most Wednesdays I hear what people say. I'm doing my best to concentrate." Todd was left to think about what had happened for the remainder of the session, as the leaders deliberately interacted with other group members and ignored him. The focus shifted to Mario when he told the group another story – this time he was sleeping in his closet. Each time Mario told a strange story, the group tried to respond with support, but could not contain their amusement. However, Todd took his plight quite seriously and repeated several times: "Mario, you're a man now, not a boy. Tell your mom that you're a man. Don't do kid's stuff, do adult stuff." Todd had again taken the role of empathic helper, saving his reputation in the group by offering words of consolation and with full concentration.

Todd slipped back into a pattern that got him into trouble in the previous session. He decided to try a "one-upmanship" strategy with Alan, one of the quieter group members who rarely spoke until now, as to which of their two family situations was most tragic. This time, both leaders were ready to confront him and, surprisingly, so was Alan.

Alan:	"Sometimes I have problems with my brother and sister."
Todd:	"At least you see them."
Alan:	"Not always, just on holidays."

Here was another situation where a group member of fairly meek mannerisms was confronting Todd on his lack of sensitivity: "Well, ah, sometimes I feel that you're not paying attention, that you're shrugging me off. Let's say you're talking and I cut you off, you wouldn't appreciate it." The pressure was even more intense than in the previous encounter with Mario, as Alan was more articulate and less anxious about Todd's reaction. Todd was *exasperated*: "Just say so if you all don't want me in the group." No one let up. Alex pointed out how Todd's reaction was a ploy to digress from the feedback. Todd seemed to accept the point when Alex reminded him that at times his family members were also frustrated with his attention-seeking annoyances. Todd's last words to the group were mixed with acknowledgement and defensiveness: "Sorry about what I did, but that's how I feel." By the next week, Todd had graciously accepted the feedback, at least outwardly: "I'm not mad about it. I'm not interrupting now, I'm OK."

Todd proved his growth over the next several sessions. His speech was more measured, and he carefully checked in with the leaders before proceeding into territory that might be deemed "interrupting." His attentiveness to the others was, as it always had been, higher than any other group member and he reiterated with great frequency how important it was to him to be helpful. Todd was also less invested in staying in a tragic spotlight and allowed room for the others to reveal their sorrows. While Todd continued, at times, his trademark question "What does that mean?", it was delivered with less investment in getting an answer. When praised for his improvement in listening to others, Todd brushed it aside with some embarrassment as he so often did: "I just want to be part of the group, but if I'm not, I'll leave."

Conclusion

Once the project was finished there was a tremendous amount for the group leaders to process, not so much about the individuals who had participated but because of the level of intimacy attained amongst those of us who served as leaders. We had shared aspects of our own lives with the group members, had close encounters with each other while strategizing on tactics, and had vehemently disagreed at times about how the project was progressing. We were also unaccustomed to dealing with developmentally disabled persons at the level of intensity required, and had to discard many of the old patterns of communication that had served us well as behavior modification counselors. We had embarked on a new level of interaction in which the old rules faded in prominence and could no longer provide the structure we had come to depend on. We had adopted a somewhat subversive stance, one that felt risky, yet there was no turning back. We encouraged each other to continue probing, and to adopt genuine dialogue within our circle. We came to the conclusion that much of what was happening in the field of developmental disabilities was left largely unexamined and generally governed by policies and procedures rather than exploration and risk-taking.

We all suffered with varying degrees of professional pride under such close scrutiny of our work and became acutely aware of the desire to shine in front of our colleagues and clients. I had the awkward role of being both a co-therapist and supervisor of the project. This meant that there were times when I gave negative feedback to other therapists, and I was also the recipient when it was my turn to conduct a group. So often in agencies that provide services to persons with developmental disabilities the staff work in isolation with the client and lack all forms of clinical supervision, particularly with those clients who live independently in the community. And while we were appreciative of the funding we had been granted to run the project, the level of tension amongst us could be overwhelming and, occasionally, sparked heated debate. At the same time, the comradeship that developed was among the most satisfying of any work experience either before or since the inception of the project. Essentially, we stood alone on an island, bucking the system, and more often than not, threatening others who were entrenched in "service provision", the old style. We faced the curious onlookers who wondered what exactly was going on behind the doors where we held the groups. We had to look after each other professionally and sometimes, personally, sensitive to the added stress the group project imposed. And we laughed continuously at ourselves, at our clients, at life. The degree of hilarity was relatively high considering the serious nature of the work – it became a way of coping with the endless tragedy that we listened to and a means of meeting the absurdity that life delivers to us all. We began to know each other at a deep level, one that evoked compassion, respect, and admiration for the courage it took to put ourselves "out there." We enjoyed the different styles with which we approached the work, such as Jesse's intelligence and ability to confront, Marco's creativity and sensitivity, Alex for his insightful observations and calm manner, and Lana's kindness, as well as her dogged persistence to work with whatever feedback she received.

We noticed that the groups developed cohesiveness at different paces and that Harold's group in particular, did so very quickly, such that Dr. Shapero deemed it a near "perfect" process. This group demonstrated an ability to both hear feedback from the leaders and deliver it to fellow participants while maintaining a dialogue entrenched in the present, in what was happening in the room right then and there. While not all members were actively involved by the end of the first month, all had shown some vulnerability in the group and it appeared to be an important, safe place to them, so much so that many arrived early; by the second session, no one was late or had missed being there. The other interesting development in this group had to do with the identification of the group member's recognition of their posturing for a position of importance. Harold in particular, was interested in assuming a role of assistant therapist and was really quite astute at giving feedback and challenging the others. By week five, several participants felt comfortable giving the "assistant therapist" a taste of his own feedback and were relieved to see Harold suffer through the process in the same way that they had! The participant who I had least expected to begin that challenge started out session six with a very forward and blunt description of Harold's lack of eye contact. She pursued a serious discussion with him in which he eventually revealed how nervous he was around others. The level of intimacy that she achieved in those few moments was more meaningful, and perhaps more in-depth, than we had achieved with him earlier.

How the groups developed as a unit, undulating in one direction and then another was something I continually questioned, particularly as it pertained to what we chose to address and how the process unfolded. For example, it became relevant when for two sessions running two men in one of the groups denied that they were ever angry. Even though one had challenged the other's denial of anger, by the next week, he too claimed "I never feel angry." While both claimed to be free of anger for different reasons, it seemed that their resistance was really a means of challenging the authority of the leaders. Once we were able to explore that process with the help of other group members, the communication began to flow.

Another interesting process was the way in which each participant increased their level of intimacy within the group and which of the exchanges were helpful in achieving an exchange on an intimate level. For example, a number of passive individuals were able to acknowledge their reticence to talk and offer meaningful explanation as to why they were "waiting for permission to speak". Often without realizing it, family members and caregivers speak for persons who are developmentally disabled to such an extent that individuals hold back, assuming that their input is secondary and unwanted. Thus it was no surprise to encounter a wall of silence encasing many of the group members, even those with well-developed verbal skills.

We had been warned by Dr. Shapero that too much intensity was detrimental to group process and I was certainly convinced that when Harold proceeded to berate others with caustic remarks, irreversible damage had occurred. Interestingly, he did not run away in spite of the fact that the majority of the group resolutely and vehemently opposed his comments. That session was the most emotionally taxing one that I had yet to participate in, and we were particularly flustered and confused about how to proceed. We knew that as leaders, we had not done enough to stop Harold and that the others would feel unsupported, perhaps even betrayed. The group dynamic shifted in significant ways after Harold's outburst of negativity. Those who were quiet began to speak and this time, without needing permission from the leaders; not only did they begin to find their voices, they also shared intimate stories about their lives and allowed us to see into their hearts. I was surprised at how quickly this process followed on the heels of the lambasting by Harold and then realized that his downfall had left a gap that the others felt confident to fill. It was also gratifying to see that they felt supported enough by us to continue to want to grow, to push on, in spite of the pain they had incurred because of our initial failure to adequately communicate to Harold. The group continued to strengthen and eventually, demonstrated adept skill and courage in their handling of Harold. When Harold blatantly lied to all of them, they were not caught off guard and appeared prepared to take him on. They could have humiliated him and shown little regard for his feelings, and with some justification, but instead maintained a firm and assertive composure. As predicted, the position of leader was soon adopted by a group member named Len, who directed most of the session and clearly put Harold in his place. Without saying so the group deferred to their new leader and complied with some of his suggestions, collaborating with his plan to deal with Harold. The rivalry between Len and Harold for top position became clear when during session ten both were trying to decide whether or not one of the group members should confront his neglectful parents; it was an interesting dialogue as they both took credit for having the greatest influence, best idea, and most prominent position in the eyes of the leaders.

After a two-week break, due to the Christmas holidays, there were significant changes in the group, the most striking being that Harold decided to leave. The group was now operating with only six members, which became problematic as only three of them were very actively verbal. There were some positive changes as well, in that those participants who had presented as self-effacing now emerged with a voice that had meaning. Eventually, we added two new members, hoping to ease the stress and achieve cohesiveness once again. One of the members was in the middle of fighting a court battle on a domestic violence charge with a former boyfriend, and was very fragile and frightened. She surprised me by telling the whole story to the group within the first half hour; I had expected that she would need some time before confessing anything personal. The second individual was clearly, and understandably, nervous and watched the entire session without saying a word. Jesse and I failed to attend to him in any way, not even acknowledging that he was there. We were too reticent about scaring him off and made the mistake of going to the other extreme. Examples of this type demonstrated to us that "staff", without input from others, can blame their "clients" for their lack of skill; this is particularly easy to do with developmentally disabled persons who have had it made clear to them over and over that they cannot and should not represent themselves, let alone assess the competency of their staff.

One of the most valuable skills (one that was novel to us) that emerged from the group therapy project was the ability to work in the "here-and-now" process, a therapeutic technique developed into a working model by Irvin Yalom (1995). Our initial challenge was to guide the members away from discussion outside of the group and to focus upon their relationships with each other and the group leaders. Once many of the critical norms were established in the groups, such as interpersonal confrontation, emotional expressivity, and valuing, the importance of the here-and-now was implicitly reinforced. The second phase of the here-and-now orientation was process illumination – a task that group members resisted early on. Initially, the group relied on the therapists to discuss process as it was too risky for any of the group members to note lack of progress, or remark if no one was disclosing. While here-and-now interaction can become part of the group norm with relative ease, process illumination was far more difficult to establish. There were many ways to recognize process such as: observing who spoke first, who sat where, which members sat together, who sat close to the therapists, who was on time or late, who spoke to whom, and who spoke not at all. In our assessment of the process, we had to pay attention to the tensions that were presented, such as the struggle for dominance and the desire to be part of the group while still maintaining one's individuality. For example, we noticed that if one group member received positive feedback from either the group leader or a peer, the others reacted, at times, with feelings akin to sibling rivalry. Our role was to search for ways to inspire the group members to notice, analyze, and speak about process.

We noticed during one of the other groups' process that we had to work diligently to keep their stories on topics in the here-and-now. Several of the group members had previous social connections with each other so the temptation to talk about the past was strong; the ties to the past also had great influence on who looked at whom, who listened to whom, and who gained control within the group. The social microcosm that emerged reminded me somewhat of a high school clique. There was a "cool" one who captured the admiration of several others, a nerd type whom everyone pitied but stayed away from, and a shy "wallflower" whose inexperience in relationships seemed obvious to the men. I observed a level of sexual tension between the men and the women in the script that seemed to be particularly strong and played out in interesting ways. The two men in the group always sat together and regularly whispered to each other like two commentators on what they saw was happening. There were other pairings in this group as well: two of the women seemed to have the classic love-hate dynamic and there may have been sexual attraction from one to the other (although it never appeared to be mutual), and two of the elderly women, although very different in personality, shared some commonalities about themes of loss including the death of family members and loneliness. One of the greatest fascinations about this group process was related to the behavior, in particular, of one member whose ability to capture the mood of the group and the subtle nuances was remarkable. He did not appear in the traditional sense to be a leader, but his quiet, unassuming manner emerged as a powerful interpreter of process. I began to regard him as a barometer – the key to unfolding the here-and-now moments and the translator of what was, at times, cryptic dialogue. His insights remained critical to the group process, perhaps too critical in the eyes of the leaders. There were sessions when his behavior either moved the group forward, or held it back until we, as leaders, decided that no one in the group should carry that much power. It was not until we received feedback from Dr. Shapero that we were "not working to capacity" that I began to realize what was happening. I was too professionally captivated, too fascinated in studying one group member who was shining – I began to lose my focus, my role in the group. I attributed this to never having witnessed the level of emotional depth present from one of the members in my previous 16 years of working with developmentally disabled persons. I was in awe. Nonetheless, I had to shift my focus from observer to leader when I realized that my regard was detrimental to the other participants, particularly in their lack of participation.

The other area of difficulty that continued to pose a problem was the strong bonds of attractions that were constantly emerging, especially between three pairs of individuals. I was not very skilled at exposing these tensions and feelings and working with them to the advantage of the group. Despite "sexuality training", I was still uncomfortable with romantic intentions surfacing from persons with developmental disabilities. What is it about the idea of a sexual encounter between two individuals with developmental disabilities that sends everyone into a panic: staff, administrators, and family members? This peculiar resistance seems to linger alongside our own personal fixations, hang-ups, confusions, projections, and longings regarding sexuality. Perhaps it is because so many view the person with a developmental disability as a perpetual child, regardless of their chronological age. We may vociferously argue for "dignity of risk" and promotion of adult-like independence but when it comes to acknowledging sexuality, most of us regress even in the face of liberal policies that carry all the right language for sexual freedom. I began to see that I was guilty in this regard by noticing my pattern to avoid powerful sexual undercurrents and persist on other topics, even if there were insignificant. I was frustrated with the lack of verbal intimacy this group was missing, and was confused as to why there were such strong feelings between them. Eventually, my co-leader Marco and I decided that unless we confronted our own shortcomings, lack of experience, and fears, we would never achieve any depth of intimacy in the group. By session nine, we were there, we had finally dealt with some of the strong feelings of attraction in a way that the group accepted and it seemed that we had struggled over an important hurdle.

As well, there was energy to this group that I liked; I used to feel optimistic about my work after the sessions ended. There was a less tragic ring to this group compared to the second one with which I was involved; perhaps my own needs were getting in the way of looking at the darker, negative feelings that surfaced, that we all carry. Many times Marco and I were lost during sessions of complex emotional entanglement that took some sorting out before we understood what had happened. The group had, even by week ten, escaped my ability to fully judge the undercurrents in critical themes and seemed stuck for a long time with only flickers of progress when someone would occasionally share a feeling but, more often than not, Marco and I felt that we were working far too hard. Wai Yung Lee had once told us that if we were applying ourselves more persistently than our clients were on their "problems", then these relationships were out of balance, that we were assuming too much responsibility. The attendance in the group began to falter and there were some weeks when only three or four members arrived. Our dialogue began to take on a perfunctory tone; I felt frustrated and bored, and angry. It was definitely one of the low points in the project for me and when one of the more vocal women dropped out, I felt discouraged about whether we would ever be able to keep the group alive.

Certainly though, the group had made some progress and there were encouraging moments that emerged as each member slowly talked about their difficulties. For example, Adam eventually revealed to the group that he suffered from muscular dystrophy. His openness, after six months of secrecy on this topic, surprised me and I realized how important it was that he talk about his own pain, rather than interpret everyone else's, which he so often did. However, it was not long before he suddenly disappeared with no explanation to any of us. His counselor later revealed to me that Adam had said he did not want to return to the group because of the "dangers and speaking one's mind". Other members also began to disappear once the key players in the group were clearly not returning and, eventually, this group ended prematurely. I became more acutely aware of how my agenda for success was an integral and, at times, negative force. My frustration with the members' inability to sustain the group probably led to discouragement for those participants who continued to arrive week after week surrounded by empty chairs. I realized that for people who are rarely given a forum to speak, who have been silenced by prejudice, silenced because they were not seen to be capable of normal emotion and silenced by low expectations, that learning to interact using genuine discourse involved a long process.

In the end, we asked for feedback, affording the participants a rare opportunity to evaluate their service provider without reprisal. So often, the feedback process for the client in a system is a perfunctory exercise in which they are put in the awkward position of being given a "say" yet have to be concerned about the risk in speaking out. Because the groups had a definite end time and none of the group leaders had dual roles, such as that of primary counselor, the clients were less restrained to share their thoughts and feelings about what had transpired. We were not naïve to the fact that all restraints were lifted; we recognized that the feedback process would take courage. Some of the comments from those group participants who felt significant improvement tended to be overwhelmingly enthusiastic: "I love these groups, honest to God!"; "In some ways this group helps me a lot. It helps me to talk"; "Sometimes it's been good to get stuff off my chest"; "I like the kind of talk – it's good"; "Kind of let go of your feelings here." Interestingly, one of the participants who indicated "no change" was cheerful about, if not proud of, the fact that she was the same as ever! I was thrilled that she felt safe enough to tell us how little she had gotten from the experience, that her genuine dislike for the group was honestly portrayed, rather than a scripted answer, those that are so often composed for people who are marginalized.

The film *One Flew over the Cuckoo's Nest* captured the chilling realization that the control, manipulation, and eventual destruction of any individual can be easily achieved by a helping professional under the rubric of "in their best interests". McMurphy, the protagonist in the film, is inadvertently admitted to a mental institution as a means of escaping a prison sentence, only to discover that the nurse/therapist on duty is a prison guard in her own right, determined to ensure his conformity to the rules regardless of their detrimental effects. His rebellion costs him his life. One is never really sure whether a strict adherence to a posture of compliance would have ultimately achieved his freedom. What is disconcerting about the portrayal of Nurse Ratchet, the head nurse on the ward, is her soft voice, fixed smile, therapeutic jargon, expressions of caring and impeccable behavior, a vessel full of well-intentioned rhetoric that paradoxically mirrors the shadow side of the human service worker. The social worker is often sanctioned with power, though often feeling powerless, a tension that seductively characterizes and consumes the worker–client relationship. This is not to suggest that social workers have an innate tendency or propensity for immorality, rather that the nature of the work itself can foster inequity. No doubt, front-line workers have an exhausting role to perform. Not only are they expected to meet the never-ending needs of their clients, they must present as patient, calm, tolerant, restrained, cheerful, and sacrificing. The pressure of maintaining a "saintly presentation", a professional stance, erodes away at genuine discourse, often leaving the staff bereft of feeling, exhibiting classic burned out symptoms. Perhaps the most dangerous aspect of social work is the denial, hypocrisy, and double binds that constantly present themselves in the day-to-day in a sense of helping. Social workers face the difficult dilemma of seeking advocacy for their clients while being accountable to a system that does not necessarily uphold client rights. Social work is one of the few professions in which *the mission* is social justice, one in which doing "good" has been professionalized, standardized, and legitimized. It is a field embedded in the culture of tragedy and disadvantage, characterized by one tale of injustice after another, only to be remedied by the well-intentioned, zealous efforts of its missionaries – the social worker. Yet, ultimately the systems that support the infrastructure of social work uphold inequities between the client and worker under the guise of empowering marginalized populations.

As was seen in the group therapy project, the group members were well aware that their position relative to the leaders was secondary and it took considerable effort and training for us to relinquish our control. Paradoxically, the stated goal that social work is about helping people can sometimes steer social workers in a direction that encourages and fosters a type of practice to the detriment of their clients. The profession extorts its academic status in the terrain of commitment to "those in need". Despite all of these proclamations, though seemingly noble and honorable, social work systems inherently establish a hierarchy entrenched in dichotomy. Indeed, the desire to empower emphasizes powerlessness, rendering the client vulnerable and dependent upon the social worker. And the systems of social work are such that staff are expected to solve the ills of society with little to no appreciation. Once the circumstances of the client are pathologized, the individuals themselves are also pathologized; how then is it possible to attribute the client with genuine emotion? By expressing pity, even compassion for our clients, we expect in return gracious cooperation and gratitude. Often, the client is then in the dubious position of having to comply with staff in order to beat the system and gain whatever advantages they can. The social workers' need for the client to change, in order to reflect success, precludes whether or not authentic relationships were upheld. Rather than acknowledging our shadow side, we prefer to exonerate ourselves as pure in motive, all the while discussing the client's problems endlessly. As long as we assume the illusory mission of reform, liberation, and justice rather than partaking in a journey that reveals our own vulnerabilities, even a lack of worth, we can never accept the scope of our client's humaneness.

It has been many years since I participated in the group therapy project and I often think back on it, amazed at what was experienced and learned. When people hear that I used to work with developmentally disabled persons, there is usually a sigh of hesitancy often followed by "How could you do that for so long?" and a general discomfort about what to say or ask. If I begin to explain that the work was initially very mundane until I realized how shallow my interactions were, and that this was *the* contributing factor to the boredom, I am still met with protestations about what a difficult, hopeless population the developmentally disabled must have been. Yet, contrary to what was expected as I transferred into other aspects of psychotherapy practise, such as trauma recovery, I found that the skills I had acquired from the group therapy project were invaluable; even more importantly, the belief that we are all capable of a level of connection far greater than imagined became firmly rooted in my work.

The quality of being human will never be captured by skill assessment analysis, reports, and IQ testing. Rather, we must value genuine regard, and seek it in others however painful or joyous, and engage towards a deeper understanding that transcends the superficialities of basic communication. We in the West live in a culture that values achieving, striving, and seeking the competitive edge. When we find ourselves in the company of people who are not capable of contributing to our consumer culture in the normative sense, we attempt to ensure that they become acculturated. We get excited about successfully placing developmentally disabled people in employment training centers so they can earn and spend money. And while there is merit to be found in job satisfaction and skill acquisition, ultimately each of us wishes not to be judged by our intellectual capabilities, earnings, or looks but by our capacity to transcend from ordinary to extraordinary through acceptance. Those individuals whose stories I have chronicled strived to face the fear of rejection and mustered the courage to reveal their most vulnerable selves while withholding judgment. All of us who participated in the group therapy project were to varying degrees transparent, struggling to live in the moment of just being, and relinquishing the temptation to prove ourselves. As those precious moments of honesty unfolded, each of us sighed with relief as we let our armour fall.

References

Yalom, I. D. (1989) *Love's Executioner and Other Tales of Psychotherapy.* New York, NY: Basic Books.

Yalom, I. D. (1970) *The Theory and Practice of Group Psychotherapy.* New York, NY: Basic Books.

Index